HUMAN RIGHTS
OPPOSING VIEWPOINTS®

Other Books of Related Interest

HUMAN RIGHTS
OPPOSING VIEWPOINTS ®

Laura K. Egendorf, *Book Editor*

Daniel Leone, *President*
Bonnie Szumski, *Publisher*
Scott Barbour, *Managing Editor*
Helen Cothran, *Senior Editor*

OPPOSING
VIEWPOINTS ®
SERIES

GREENHAVEN
PRESS ®

THOMSON
─────★─────™
GALE

San Diego • Detroit • New York • San Francisco • Cleveland
New Haven, Conn. • Waterville, Maine • London • Munich

LIBRARY OF CONGRESS CATALOGING-IN-PUBLICATION DATA

Human rights : opposing viewpoints / Laura K. Egendorf, book editor.
    p. cm. — (Opposing viewpoints series)
    Includes bibliographical references and index.
    ISBN 0-7377-1690-8 (pbk. : alk. paper) — ISBN 0-7377-1689-4 (lib. : alk. paper)
    1. Human rights. I. Egendorf, Laura K., 1973– .
    JC571.H76968 2003
    323—dc21
                                                        2002192800

Printed in the United States of America

"Congress shall make no law. . . abridging the freedom of speech, or of the press."

First Amendment to the U.S. Constitution

The basic foundation of our democracy is the First Amendment guarantee of freedom of expression. The Opposing Viewpoints Series is dedicated to the concept of this basic freedom and the idea that it is more important to practice it than to enshrine it.

Contents

Why Consider Opposing Viewpoints?

"The only way in which a human being can make some approach to knowing the whole of a subject is by hearing what can be said about it by persons of every variety of opinion and studying all modes in which it can be looked at by every character of mind. No wise man ever acquired his wisdom in any mode but this."

John Stuart Mill

In our media-intensive culture it is not difficult to find differing opinions. Thousands of newspapers and magazines and dozens of radio and television talk shows resound with differing points of view. The difficulty lies in deciding which opinion to agree with and which "experts" seem the most credible. The more inundated we become with differing opinions and claims, the more essential it is to hone critical reading and thinking skills to evaluate these ideas. Opposing Viewpoints books address this problem directly by presenting stimulating debates that can be used to enhance and teach these skills. The varied opinions contained in each book examine many different aspects of a single issue. While examining these conveniently edited opposing views, readers can develop critical thinking skills such as the ability to compare and contrast authors' credibility, facts, argumentation styles, use of persuasive techniques, and other stylistic tools. In short, the Opposing Viewpoints Series is an ideal way to attain the higher-level thinking and reading skills so essential in a culture of diverse and contradictory opinions.

In addition to providing a tool for critical thinking, Opposing Viewpoints books challenge readers to question their own strongly held opinions and assumptions. Most people form their opinions on the basis of upbringing, peer pressure, and personal, cultural, or professional bias. By reading carefully balanced opposing views, readers must directly confront new ideas as well as the opinions of those with whom they disagree. This is not to simplistically argue that

everyone who reads opposing views will—or should—
change his or her opinion. Instead, the series enhances readers' understanding of their own views by encouraging con-
frontation with opposing ideas. Careful examination of others' views can lead to the readers' understanding of the
logical inconsistencies in their own opinions, perspective on
why they hold an opinion, and the consideration of the possibility that their opinion requires further evaluation.

Evaluating Other Opinions

To ensure that this type of examination occurs, Opposing
Viewpoints books present all types of opinions. Prominent
spokespeople on different sides of each issue as well as well-
known professionals from many disciplines challenge the
reader. An additional goal of the series is to provide a forum
for other, less known, or even unpopular viewpoints. The
opinion of an ordinary person who has had to make the decision to cut off life support from a terminally ill relative, for
example, may be just as valuable and provide just as much insight as a medical ethicist's professional opinion. The editors
have two additional purposes in including these less known
views. One, the editors encourage readers to respect others'
opinions—even when not enhanced by professional credibility. It is only by reading or listening to and objectively evaluating others' ideas that one can determine whether they are
worthy of consideration. Two, the inclusion of such viewpoints encourages the important critical thinking skill of objectively evaluating an author's credentials and bias. This
evaluation will illuminate an author's reasons for taking a
particular stance on an issue and will aid in readers' evaluation of the author's ideas.

It is our hope that these books will give readers a deeper
understanding of the issues debated and an appreciation of
the complexity of even seemingly simple issues when good
and honest people disagree. This awareness is particularly
important in a democratic society such as ours in which
people enter into public debate to determine the common
good. Those with whom one disagrees should not be regarded as enemies but rather as people whose views deserve
careful examination and may shed light on one's own.

Thomas Jefferson once said that "difference of opinion leads to inquiry, and inquiry to truth." Jefferson, a broadly educated man, argued that "if a nation expects to be ignorant and free . . . it expects what never was and never will be." As individuals and as a nation, it is imperative that we consider the opinions of others and examine them with skill and discernment. The Opposing Viewpoints Series is intended to help readers achieve this goal.

David L. Bender and Bruno Leone,
Founders

Greenhaven Press anthologies primarily consist of previously published material taken from a variety of sources, including periodicals, books, scholarly journals, newspapers, government documents, and position papers from private and public organizations. These original sources are often edited for length and to ensure their accessibility for a young adult audience. The anthology editors also change the original titles of these works in order to clearly present the main thesis of each viewpoint and to explicitly indicate the opinion presented in the viewpoint. These alterations are made in consideration of both the reading and comprehension levels of a young adult audience. Every effort is made to ensure that Greenhaven Press accurately reflects the original intent of the authors included in this anthology.

Introduction

*"Human rights theory as we know it today [in the West]
... [flourished] and spread throughout the
Enlightenment."*

—*Fred Edwords*

Human rights, as they are understood by the modern Western world, took almost exactly one century to develop. The events responsible for formalizing the concept of human rights include the Glorious Revolution, which in 1688 brought King William and Queen Mary to the English throne; Thomas Jefferson's writing of the Declaration of Independence in 1776; the passage of the U.S. Bill of Rights in 1789; and the adoption of the Declaration of the Rights of Man and Citizen by the French Constituent Assembly, also in 1789. Those one hundred and one years coincided with the Age of Enlightenment, a time when writers and philosophers such as John Locke and Voltaire began to argue for the primacy of reason, science, and "natural rights"—rights that all people are entitled to, that cannot be taken away by any king or government. Locke and others protested intolerance, censorship, dogmatism, and anything else that limited human growth and the acquisition of knowledge.

That is not to say that the concept of human rights was nonexistent prior to 1688. For example, in 1215, the Magna Carta, signed by England's King John at the behest of his barons, guaranteed nobles the right to a jury of their peers, limited the punishments for freedmen and merchants, and established the right of all free citizens to own and inherit property. In addition, the philosophy of humanism, which emphasized the goodness and dignity of humankind, blossomed during the Renaissance in the fourteenth through sixteenth centuries.

The turning point in the ideation of human rights, however, was the Glorious (or Bloodless) Revolution, which ended the reign of King James II of England. Fearful of the Catholic king and the possibility that his Catholic son might inherit the throne, key political leaders beseeched the Dutch prince William of Orange and his wife, Mary, (King James's Protestant daughter) to come to England. They arrived with an army in November 1688 and overthrew King James, who fled to France. The next year, the Parliament passed a Bill of Rights. Although flawed by modern standards—for example, the bill banned Roman Catholics from the throne—the document made it illegal for the British monarch to impose taxes without the consent of Parliament or to suspend laws. It also prohibited excessive fines, bails, and cruel and unusual punishments.

In 1690, the man who played arguably the greatest role in the development of human rights published his essay "Of Civil Government." In that treatise, British philosopher John Locke declared, "The natural liberty of man is to be free from any superior power on earth, and not to be under the will or legislative authority of man, but to have only the law of nature for his rule." Locke also asserted that people are entitled to property and to the fruits of their labor. However, the philosopher argued that such liberties should not be accompanied by anarchy. Governments are necessary, but they are legitimate only through consent. According to Locke, the role of government is to ensure "the peace, safety, and public good of the people" while the role of citizens is to obey legitimate laws.

Locke's views found an eager audience in the American colonies, particularly during the Revolutionary War. In the Declaration of Independence, Thomas Jefferson wrote that because governments cannot rule without consent, citizens have the right to alter or abolish governments when their rights are ignored or restricted. According to Jefferson: "When a long train of abuses and usurpations, pursuing invariably the same object evinces a design to reduce [the people] under absolute despotism, it is their right, it is their duty, to throw off such government, and to provide new guards for their future security." Thirteen years later, on September 25, 1789, Congress passed the Bill of Rights, although the document did not become law until December 15, 1791, when Virginia ratified it. The rights listed in those ten amendments—freedom of speech, trial by jury, and protection against cruel and unusual punishment among them—are well known to most Americans, and they echo the values that had developed throughout the previous century. These rights also helped ensure that the goals set forth in the preamble to the constitution—"[to] promote the general welfare, and secure the blessings of liberty to ourselves and our posterity"— would be met. As Fred Edwords, the editor of *Humanist* magazine, explains, "In their completeness, these amendments constitute a definitive compilation of the best judicial thinking on individual human rights from the preceding two hundred years."

France's overthrow of its monarchy followed on the heels of America's revolution. The Declaration of the Rights of Man and Citizen was adopted on August 26, 1789. The document's authors stated: "Ignorance, disregard or contempt of the rights of man are the sole causes of public misfortunes and governmental corruption." These rights included the presumption of innocence, freedom of speech and press, freedom of religious expression—as long as that expression did not disturb the public order—and the prohibition of government seizure of property without just cause or compensation.

The concept of modern human rights has continued to evolve since the Age of Enlightenment. In 1948, just three years after World War II and the Holocaust, the United Nations ratified the Universal Declaration of Human Rights. These universal rights include the right to live in freedom, without fear of torture or slavery, the right to participate in government, the right to work, and the right to education. This ever-expanding concept of human rights has led to the creation of countless human rights organizations whose aim is to monitor the state of human rights around the world and to prevent human rights abuses.

However, not every nation appreciates the work that these organizations do. Some countries do not believe in the universality of human rights or in the primacy of the Western view. Singapore diplomat Bilahari Kausikan observes, "The hard core of rights that is truly universal is smaller than the West [has] maintained." Many people have argued that regional values must be taken into consideration and that Western Europe and North America are biased against the traditions of Latin America, Asia, and Africa. Another concern is that the West emphasizes individual rights at the expense of national cohesion. Singapore ambassador Mark Hong contends: "In my view, the West may have overprivileged the individual to the point where the rights of society are undermined."

The universality of human rights, and the role of the West in formulating those rights, continues to be hotly debated. The state of human rights in the world today, and the best ways to guarantee those rights, are also of interest to countless scholars, politicians, and humanitarian organizations. In *Human Rights: Opposing Viewpoints*, the contributors explore human rights in the following chapters: How Should Human Rights Be Defined? What Is the State of Human Rights? What Should Be Done to Stop Human Rights Abuses? How Should the United States Respond to Crimes Against Humanity? In attempting to answer these questions, the authors illustrate that while human rights may have blossomed more than two centuries ago, the discussion about them has yet to wither.

CHAPTER 1

How Should Human Rights Be Defined?

Chapter Preface

Human rights are generally understood to fall into two categories. The first category, civil and political rights, includes freedom of expression, freedom to participate in government, and equality before the law. The second category of rights encompasses economic, social, and cultural freedoms, such as the right to work, the freedom to participate in cultural life, and the right to an adequate standard of living. Although American commentators have disagreed on the relative importance of each set of rights, political and civil rights are generally understood to take precedence over economic, social, and cultural rights. This belief may be due to the fact that Western nations tend to emphasize civil and political freedoms. For instance, the U.S. Constitution and its amendments contain paragraphs detailing the frequency of elections and establishing rights such as freedom of speech and trial by jury. However, no mention is made of minimum wages or access to social services. In contrast, non-Western nations, especially in Asia, often emphasize the secondary category of rights.

Many in the West perceive economic, social, and cultural rights to be less important than civil and political rights despite the fact that such rights are mentioned in the United Nations' Universal Declaration of Human Rights. Article 22 reads:

> Everyone, as a member of society, has the right to social security and is entitled to realization . . . of the economic, social and cultural rights indispensable for his dignity and the free development of his personality.

Despite Article 22, the secondary nature of these three rights is longstanding. Thomas Hammarberg, the UN Secretary-General's Special Representative for Human Rights in Cambodia, writes that when the Universal Declaration was formulated in 1948, many Americans and others "argued that 'Freedom from Want,' to use the language of President Franklin D. Roosevelt, should not be seen as a human right." Eighteen years later, the United Nations issued two separate "International Covenants"—one on civil and political rights, the other on economic, social, and cultural rights. According to Hammarberg, "The fact that it was not possible to keep all these rights within the same package perpetuated the perception that they were different in nature, that economic and social rights were secondary."

Hammarberg and others contend that these two categories of rights must be considered interrelated. Shulamith Koenig, the executive director of the People's Decade for Human Rights Education, asserts: "In a society where basic survival needs are not met, civil and political rights are meaningless if an individual must first be concerned with obtaining adequate food, shelter, and health care." Likewise, the reverse is true: When civil and political rights are neglected, economic, social, and cultural conditions can suffer. Hammarberg states, "It is now widely recognized that economic growth and eradication of poverty indeed are encouraged by free discussion and the role of law." When political and civil rights are absent, people encounter economic, social, and cultural difficulties. He claims, for example, that studies have shown links between censorship and famine in South Asia.

While the existence of a Universal Declaration of Human Rights might indicate otherwise, the world has yet to agree on one universal standard of human rights or the relative importance of economic, social, and cultural rights. To be sure, different countries have different priorities. For some nations, economic growth might take precedence over concerns about child labor while other countries might emphasize individual rights over social cohesion. These regional values often take supremacy over universal mores, which makes defining human rights more difficult. In the following chapter, the authors debate how human rights should best be defined.

> "The possibility of justifiable modifications
> . . . must not obscure the fundamental
> universality of international human rights
> norms."

Human Rights Are Universal

Jack Donnelly

In the following viewpoint, Jack Donnelly argues that while some modifications may be justifiable, human rights are a universal concept that must be respected among all cultures. He disputes the idea that developing nations are unable to embrace civil and political rights because of their traditional values. According to Donnelly, such extreme relativist views cannot be supported because everyone is entitled to certain rights, including the rights of life and liberty and protection against slavery and torture. Donnelly is a professor at the University of Denver's Graduate School of International Studies and the author of *International Human Rights*, the source of the following viewpoint.

As you read, consider the following questions:
1. What is the Second World approach to human rights, as stated by the author?
2. According to Donnelly, what is radical universalism?
3. Why does the author believe that the Muslim law that requires women to wear veils in public is compatible with human rights?

Jack Donnelly, *International Human Rights*. Boulder, CO: Westview Press, 1998. Copyright © 1998 by Westview Press, a member of the Perseus Books Group. Reproduced by permission.

[R]elativists argue] that moral values are historically or culturally specific rather than universal. For example, [George F.] Kennan argued that "there are no internationally accepted standards of morality to which the U.S. government could appeal if it wished to act in the name of moral principles.". . .

The "Three Worlds" of Rights

It is often claimed that there are a variety of distinctive and defensible conceptions of human rights that merit our respect and toleration even if we disagree with them. One standard form of this argument, which was particularly prominent in the 1980s, was the claim that there are "three worlds" of human rights. The "Western" (First World) approach, it is asserted, emphasizes civil and political rights and the right to private property. The "socialist" (Second World) approach emphasizes economic and social rights. The "Third World" approach emphasizes self-determination and economic development. Furthermore, both the socialist and the Third World conceptions are held to be group oriented, in contrast to the fundamental individualism of the "Western" approach.

The reality of Western practice over the past half century, however, has been quite different. The West may have neglected economic and social rights in the nineteenth and early twentieth centuries. But that anyone looking at the welfare states of Western Europe over the past half century can be expected to take such a description of the Western approach seriously, to put it bluntly, boggles the mind. In fact, the liberal democratic welfare states of Western (and especially northern) Europe are the countries that have taken most seriously the interdependence and indivisibility of all human rights. And it is in these countries that we find the most complete realization of internationally recognized economic, social, and cultural rights.

Conversely, as we saw in 1989, citizens in the former Soviet bloc, when given the opportunity, demanded their civil and political rights. Far from being a superfluous bourgeois luxury, Eastern Europeans no less than Western Europeans see civil and political rights as essential to a life of dignity. And the dismal state of Soviet bloc economies suggests that the sacrifice of civil and political rights probably did not even facilitate the long-term realization of economic and social rights.

The recent wave of liberalizations and democratizations likewise suggests that the so-called Third World conception of human rights has little basis in local values. Ordinary citizens in country after country have found that internationally recognized civil and political rights are essential to protecting themselves against repressive economic and political elites. When given the chance, they have in effect declared that sacrifices made in the name of development, self-determination, or national security were not chosen but were imposed through force and the systematic violation of civil and political rights.

Political histories, cultural legacies, economic conditions, and human rights problems certainly differ in these three "worlds." For that matter, there is considerable diversity even within each "world," especially the Third World. Cultural relativity is a fact. Social institutions and values have varied, and continue to vary, with time and place. Nonetheless, I will argue that contemporary international human rights norms have near universal applicability, requiring only relatively modest adjustments in the name of cultural diversity.

Relativism and Universalism

Moral relativism, the belief that moral values (and thus conceptions of human rights) are determined by history, culture, economics, or some other independent social force, is best seen as a matter of degree. At one extreme is a radical relativism that sees culture (or history, or economics) as the source of all values. Such a position in effect denies the very idea of human rights, for it holds that there are no rights that everyone is entitled to equally, simply as a human being. Radical relativism can be ignored once we have decided, as we have above, that there *are* human rights, rights that all human beings have, independent of society (and thus irrespective of their particular history or culture).

At the other end of the spectrum lies radical universalism, the view that all values, including human rights, are entirely universal, in no way subject to modification in light of cultural or historical differences. In its pure form, radical universalism would hold that there is only one set of human rights that applies at all times and in all places. But to insist that all human rights be implemented in identical ways in all countries would be wildly unrealistic, and most people would find such a demand morally and politically perverse. Rejecting the two end points of the spectrum leaves us with a considerable variety of "relativist" positions, which can be roughly divided into two ranges. *Strong relativism* holds that human rights (and other values) are principally, but not entirely, determined by culture or other circumstances. "Universal" human rights serve as a check on culturally specific values. The emphasis, however, is on variation and relativity. *Weak relativism* reverses the emphasis. Universal human rights are held to be subject only to secondary cultural modifications. I will defend a form of weak cultural relativism on both descriptive and prescriptive grounds.

The Most Important Rights

Internationally recognized human rights represent a good first approximation of the guarantees necessary for a life of dignity in the contemporary world of modern states and modern markets. In all countries, the unchecked power of the modern state threatens individuals, families, groups, and communities alike. Likewise, national and international markets, whether free or controlled, threaten human dignity in all countries. The [1966 Universal Declaration of Human Rights] and the [1976 International Covenant on Civil and Political Rights and the International Covenant on Economic, Social and Cultural Rights] provide a generally sound approach to protecting human dignity against these threats.

For example, it is difficult to imagine defensible arguments in the contemporary world to deny rights to life, liberty, security of the person, or protection against slavery, arbitrary arrest, racial discrimination, and torture. The rights to food, health care, work, and social insurance are equally basic to any plausible conception of equal human dignity.

Universality, however, is only an initial presumption. Deviations from international human rights norms may be justified, even demanded. For example, the free and full consent of spouses in marriage (Universal Declaration, Article 16) reflects a culturally specific conception of marriage that would be unreasonable to apply everywhere without exception. This does not mean that we should approve of forced marriages. It does, however, suggest that we tolerate some notions of consent that would be unacceptable in the contemporary West.

Hiding Behind Traditions

Those who champion the view that human rights are not universal frequently insist that their adversaries have hidden agendas. In fairness, the same accusation can be leveled against at least some of those who cite culture as a defense against human rights. Authoritarian regimes who appeal to their own cultural traditions are cheerfully willing to crush culture domestically when it suits them to do so. Also, the "traditional culture" that is sometimes advanced to justify the nonobservance of human rights, including in Africa, in practice no longer exists in a pure form at the national level anywhere. The societies of developing countries have not remained in a pristine, pre-Western state; all have been subject to change and distortion by external influence, both as a result of colonialism in many cases and through participation in modern interstate relations.

You cannot impose the model of a "modern" nation-state cutting across tribal boundaries and conventions on your country, appoint a president and an ambassador to the United Nations, and then argue that tribal traditions should be applied to judge the human rights conduct of the resulting modern state.

Shashi Tharoor, *World Policy Journal*, Winter 1999–2000.

The possibility of justifiable modifications, however, must not obscure the fundamental universality of international human rights norms. Deviations should be rare. And the need to keep their cumulative impact minor suggests that substantial variations are likely to be legitimate only in relatively specific and detailed matters of implementation.

Allowing for Variations

We can distinguish three levels at which the substance of a human right can be specified. At the top are what we can call

23

"concepts," very general formulations such as the rights to political participation or work. Little cultural variability at this level is justifiable. Below these are what we can call "interpretations." For example, a guaranteed job and unemployment insurance are two interpretations of the right to work. Some interpretative variability seems plausible for most internationally recognized human rights. And at a still more detailed third level, there is room for considerable variation in the particular form in which an interpretation is implemented.

Suppose that we interpret the right to political participation as a right to vote in open and fair elections. Members of the legislature might be chosen through winner-take-all elections in local districts or by a system in which people vote for party lists and seats in the legislature are awarded proportional to the national vote. Such variations of form should usually be considered permissible, as long as they tend to realize a defensible interpretation of the governing concept.

These guidelines will not provide clear answers in all important cases. They do, however, have strong and generally clear implications. . . . To illustrate my argument here, I want to consider the claim of many religious fundamentalists, especially among monotheistic revealed religions of the Near East (Judaism, Christianity, and Islam), that men and women do not have the same rights, that each sex has its own particular, and largely complementary, social and political rights and responsibilities.

The weak relativist position sketched above would reject such an argument. The claim that because of ascriptive characteristics such as age, sex, race, or family one is not entitled to the same basic human rights as members of other groups is incompatible with the very idea of human rights. This does not imply that all differences based on gender are incompatible with human rights. For example, dress codes to protect public morals and decency, such as the Muslim requirement that women wear veils in public or the Western requirement that women (but not men) cover their chests in public, clearly lie within the realm of permissible distinctions. But the claim that one group in society has radically different basic rights from another group—for example, that it can deny the rights to vote, speak, and assemble freely to women, deny women full and equal legal personality, or award otherwise identical men and women different treatment in social insurance schemes—is not a culturally different conception of human rights but a (partial) rejection of the very idea of *human* rights.

Human rights do not require cultural homogenization. If women *choose* to vote as their husbands do or choose a private family life instead of a public life and work outside of the home, human rights require that such choices be respected. But when they are imposed—and especially when those who define and enforce differential rights receive preferred treatment—they involve unacceptable violations of human rights.

Such an argument does not imply wanton cultural imperialism. The legacy of imperialism demands that Westerners in particular show special caution and sensitivity when dealing with clashing cultural values. Caution, however, must not be confused with inaction. Even if we are not entitled to impose our values on others, they are our own values. Sometimes they may demand that we act on them even in the absence of agreement by others. And if the practices of others are particularly objectionable—consider, for example, societies in which it is traditional to kill the first-born child if it is female or the deeply rooted tradition of anti-Semitism in the West—even strongly sanctioned traditions may deserve neither our respect nor our toleration.

VIEWPOINT

*"Much of the developing world views the
[Universal Declaration of Human Rights]
as . . . not necessarily applicable to their
own communities."*

Human Rights Are Not Necessarily Universal

Blair Gibb

In the following viewpoint, Blair Gibb asserts that the rights established by the 1948 Universal Declaration of Human Rights (UDHR) may not be relevant for all nations. According to Gibb, several Asian nations have contended that the individual freedoms set forth in the UDHR do not apply to their societies, which emphasize economic development and social cohesion over individualism and freedom of speech. He maintains that this Asian view on human rights stands in contrast to the U.S. model, which, by its emphasis on individual rights, has led to numerous problems, such as extremes of wealth and poverty. Many Asian nations reject this tradeoff as too costly, Gibb contends. Prior to his death in 1999, Gibb was a planning officer for Amnesty International and the coauthor of *When Good Companies Do Bad Things.*

As you read, consider the following questions:
1. Why do some human rights advocates fear "cultural particularity," as stated by the author?
2. In Gibb's opinion, what are the consequences of the U.S. model of human rights?
3. Why does the author believe Europeans are better suited than Americans when it comes to understanding the multicultural nature of human rights?

Blair Gibb, "Global Aspirations, Local Gospels," *Whole Earth*, Summer 1999.
Copyright © 1999 by *Whole Earth*. Reproduced by permission of Point
Foundation.

M ost of the human-rights standards which now exist in international law ultimately derive from the international teachings of the world's major religions/philosophies. The presumption of innocence comes from ancient Islamic law; [Chinese philosopher] Confucius devoted great attention to the obligations of a sovereign toward his people; and the Judeo-Christian "golden rule"—the idea of reciprocal obligations, responsibilities, and respect—has shaped the fundamental standards of behavior of most cultures.

The Importance of the Universal Declaration of Human Rights

The standards we now call "rights" were formalized over centuries in various national legal systems. In the twentieth century these understandings have been codified in several major international conventions agreed to by a majority of the world's nations, starting with the Slavery Convention of 1926 [which labeled slavery a "crime against humanity"]. The most important of these is the Universal Declaration of Human Rights (UDHR), proclaimed in 1948 by the founding members of the United Nations. The preamble to the UDHR calls for its provisions to be promoted and supported by "every organ of society," which presumably includes business.

The UDHR, while inescapably a political document in the sense that it was the product of the concerns and agendas of particular nations at a particular time, has, since 1948, defined the frontiers and terms of the various debates over human rights. It contains thirty principles, which include not only civil and political rights, but economic, social, and cultural rights as well.

Civil and political rights include the rights to freedom of religion, freedom of association, freedom from torture and slavery, freedom from discrimination, and the right to participate in government through the electoral process. Economic, cultural, and social rights include the right to education, the right to just and favorable conditions of work, and the right to participate in cultural life.

Most of the rights and freedoms in the convenants may be limited by national governments—for example, in times of national emergency. However, there are certain rights that are "nonderogable"—in other words, under international law, no state can limit or deny them under any circumstances. These include:

Right to life; Right to recognition as a person before the law; Freedom of thought, conscience, and religion; Freedom from torture; Freedom from slavery; Freedom from imprisonment for debt or from retroactive penal legislation.

Most of these international agreements have the tone of statements of aspiration rather than reality—the way we would like the world to be, rather than the way it usually is. But collective aspirations are important statements and have played a powerful role in human history. Without them, there would still be millions of human beings sold into slavery, burned or hanged as witches, and victimized by other practices that the vast majority of us now rightly reject.

The Controversy of Universality

Lurking behind the definitional issue of human rights is the complex and controversial problem of whether human rights are "universal" or just "Western" values. The UDHR, of course, states that the freedoms and rights it contains are universal and apply to all human beings by virtue of their common humanity. [Philosophy professor] Dr. Morton Winston describes an Asian "challenge" to the UDHR which emerged in the Bangkok Declaration, adopted at the World Human Rights Conference Regional Preparatory meeting in 1993. Several Asian states, including Singapore, Malaysia, Indonesia, and China, refuted the notion—intrinsic to the UDHR—that human-rights standards can be "universal." The Asian countries maintained that recognition of "cultural particularities" was prerequisite to interpreting human-rights standards for international application; that their societies have different priorities and that economic development, social cohesion, and other goals are more important to them than individual freedoms. The principal objections were to what these countries considered inappropriately absolute language regarding civil and political rights, such as freedom of speech and, especially, freedom to criticize the government. Article 19, for instance, says that "everyone has the right to freedom of opinion and expression; this right includes freedom to hold opinions without interference and to seek, receive, and impart information and ideas through any media and regardless of frontiers." China's tight control of its citizens' access to the Internet, for example, would be a violation of human rights under this article.

The Confusion of Universality

The uselessness of the various UN forums on human rights is a product of the difficulties in applying the concept of the universality of human rights. This is not just a matter of the fact that there are many non-democratic states participating in the work of the UN. There is also a great deal of confusion and uncertainty as to the basis for universal human rights—are there religious, cultural, racial, gender, and other differences which suggest that human rights cannot be universal, and are exponents of universal human rights entitled to argue that somehow their notions are superior to those of others who begin from different conceptions, theistic or cultural?

Quadrant, June 1998.

As Morton Winston says, some human-rights advocates fear that consideration of "cultural particularity" might introduce a means for individual governments to pick and choose which standards apply to them. The Asian demurrals were quashed at the Vienna World Conference later that year with this insertion into the Vienna Declaration: "The universal nature of these rights and freedoms is beyond question." Nonetheless, the marker has been put down, and the ongoing shift of economic power to the East guarantees, at the very least, that the debate will continue. It has challenged the primacy of the US Model as the model of freedom.

The Problematic US Model

The US Model is the most individualistic and socially least cohesive of comparative cultures, leading to a freewheeling, heterogeneous society full of contentious pluralism, social Darwinist economic practices, and self-destructive behavior. I heard on the radio that the board of supervisors in my parents' rural county had voted down several minor recommendations for environmental regulation of oceanfront construction, having concluded that, "while the recommendations were worthwhile, they would interfere with the individual's right to do as he pleases." This may be an extreme example, but to large parts of the world, this is the American Way—unconcerned with the needs of a larger society at home, but quick to lecture other countries about their own behavior.

In the US Model, much more than in other countries, society exists to serve the individual and allow the fullest possible self-expression. Extremes of wealth and poverty, profligacy with natural resources, high crime levels, and other features of society that would be considered unacceptable elsewhere are tolerated in the US in the name of individual freedom. The creativity and economic power this tolerance has created may be a source of envy and admiration, but for many outside the US, the social price paid for these benefits simply looks too high.

In many other societies, the individual exists to serve a greater good—his or her family, clan, faith, or country. Problem solving is done not by individual heroes but by negotiation, consensus, group agreement; individuals are willing to give up a certain amount of "freedom" in return for security and relative lack of conflict. Egyptian law professor Kamal Abu al-Magd has observed, "The chances for the effective protection of human rights should be greater if you have a community of individuals competing to fulfill obligations rather than having a community of individuals fighting selfishly for their rights."

The Values of Developing Nations

Singapore's economic growth and social cohesion are greatly admired by many developing countries. How much significance Singapore places on the obligations of the individual to the larger community was brought home to the world in 1994, when Michael Fay, a young American convicted of vandalism (spray painting graffiti on cars), was sentenced to flogging. Like many Americans who visit the Port of Singapore's headquarters building, I am struck by the rolling digital display in the elevators showing the repeated phrase, "Good character will be rewarded." Such slogans would probably be considered unbearably coercive (or worse, laughably uncynical) in a New York office building.

While the industrialized democracies consider the Universal Declaration of Human Rights a legitimate and timeless statement of "universal" values, much of the developing world views the agreement as a more limited product of negotiation and compromise among superpowers, not necessarily applicable to their own communities. Within this difference of opinion lies the seed of one of the major challenges of the future: enforcement of these rights in a genuinely multicultural context. In my experience, Europeans, without pretending to be moral exemplars but with their own memories of twentieth-century horror still alive, are more sensitive than Americans, with their notorious short memories and resulting ability to forget their own past complicities (e.g., installing and supporting repressive regimes abroad, or the extermination of indigenous Native American peoples).

Whatever de jure standards develop in the human-rights area, it is de facto standards that matter in the crunch. Whether or not the international community, or segments of it, can develop genuine methods to enforce human-rights values and protect real lives will be the defining issue for the next century.

"The right to the highest attainable standard of health . . . has been firmly endorsed in a wide range of international and regional human rights instruments."

Health Care Is a Human Right

World Health Organization

In the following viewpoint, the World Health Organization (WHO) argues that access to health care is an important human right and that health and human rights are interconnected. WHO asserts that human rights violations, such as torture, can have harmful consequences to health. Moreover, WHO claims that the design and implementation of health care policies can either improve or worsen human rights. According to the organization, nations must ensure that their health care programs are free from discrimination, readily accessible, respectful of medical ethics, and of good quality. The World Health Organization, which is the United Nations specialized agency for health, seeks to improve the quality of physical, social, and mental health around the world.

As you read, consider the following questions:

1. What are the health issues people should be educated about, in the opinion of the World Health Organization?
2. According to the May 2000 General Comment issued by the Committee on Economic, Social and Cultural Rights, what are some of the rights to which the right to health is interrelated?
3. How does discrimination relate to health, according to WHO?

World Health Organization, "Twenty-Five Questions and Answers on Health and Human Rights," *Health & Human Rights Publication Series*, July 2002, pp. 9–11, 18, 22. Copyright © 2002 by World Health Organization. Reproduced by permission.

Q.1 *What are human rights?*
Human rights are legally guaranteed by human rights law, protecting individuals and groups against actions that interfere with fundamental freedoms and human dignity.

They encompass what are known as civil, cultural, economic, political and social rights. Human rights are principally concerned with the relationship between the individual and the state. Governmental obligations with regard to human rights broadly fall under the principles of *respect, protect and fulfil.*

Q.2 How are human rights enshrined in international law?

In the aftermath of World War II, the international community adopted the Universal Declaration of Human Rights (UDHR, 1948). However, by the time that States were prepared to turn the provisions of the Declaration into binding law, the Cold War had overshadowed and polarised human rights into two separate categories. The West argued that civil and political rights had priority and that economic and social rights were mere aspirations. The Eastern bloc argued to the contrary that rights to food, health and education were paramount and civil and political rights secondary. Hence two separate treaties were created in 1966—the International Covenant on Economic, Social and Cultural Rights (ICESCR) and the International Covenant on Civil and Political Rights (ICCPR). Since then, numerous treaties, declarations and other legal instruments have been adopted, and it is these instruments that encapsulate human rights.

The Connection Between Health and Human Rights

Q.3 What is the link between health and human rights?

There are complex linkages between health and human rights:

- Violations or lack of attention to human rights can have serious health consequences;
- Health policies and programmes can promote or violate human rights in the ways they are designed or implemented;
- Vulnerability and the impact of ill health can be reduced by taking steps to respect, protect and fulfil human rights.

The normative content of each right is fully articulated in

human rights instruments. In relation to the right to health and freedom from discrimination, the normative content is outlined in Questions 4 and 5, respectively. Examples of the language used in human rights instruments to articulate the normative content of some of the other key human rights relevant to health follow:

• Torture: "No one shall be subjected to torture or to cruel, inhuman or degrading treatment or punishment. In particular, no one shall be subjected without his free consent to medical or scientific experimentation."

• Violence against children: "All appropriate legislative, administrative, social and educational measures to protect the child from all forms of physical or mental violence, injury or abuse, neglect or negligent treatment, maltreatment or exploitation, including sexual abuse . . ." shall be taken.

• Harmful traditional practices: "Effective and appropriate measures with a view to abolishing traditional practices prejudicial to the health of children" shall be taken.

• Participation: The right to ". . . active, free and meaningful participation."

• Information: "Freedom to seek, receive and impart information and ideas of all kinds."

• Privacy: "No one shall be subjected to arbitrary or unlawful interference with his privacy. . . ."

• Scientific progress: The right of everyone to enjoy the benefits of scientific progress and its applications.

• Education: The right to education, including access to education in support of basic knowledge of child health and nutrition, the advantages of breast-feeding, hygiene and environmental sanitation and the prevention of accidents.

• Food and nutrition: "The right of everyone to adequate food and the fundamental right of everyone to be free from hunger. . ."

• Standard of living: Everyone has the right to an adequate standard of living, including adequate food, clothing, housing, and medical care and necessary social services.

• Right to social security: The right of everyone to social security, including social insurance.

Q.4 What is meant by "the right to health"?
United Nations High Commissioner for Human Rights,

Mary Robinson [says], *"The right to health does not mean the right to be healthy, nor does it mean that poor governments must put in place expensive health services for which they have no resources. But it does require governments and public authorities to put in place policies and action plans which will lead to available and accessible health care for all in the shortest possible time. To ensure that this happens is the challenge facing both the human rights community and public health professionals."*

The right to the highest attainable standard of health (referred to as "the right to health") was first reflected in the WHO Constitution (1946) and then reiterated in the 1978 Declaration of Alma Ata and in the World Health Declaration adopted by the World Health Assembly in 1998.

It has been firmly endorsed in a wide range of international and regional human rights instruments.

The right to the highest attainable standard of health in international human rights law is a claim to a set of social arrangements—norms, institutions, laws, an enabling environment—that can best secure the enjoyment of this right. The most authoritative interpretation of the right to health is outlined in Article 12 of the ICESCR, which has been ratified by 145 countries (as of May 2002). In May 2000, the Committee on Economic, Social and Cultural Rights, which monitors the Covenant, adopted a General Comment on the right to health.

Four Criteria

General Comments serve to clarify the nature and content of individual rights and States Parties™ (those states that have ratified) obligations. The General Comment recognized that the right to health is closely related to and dependent upon the realization of other human rights, including the right to food, housing, work, education, participation, the enjoyment of the benefits of scientific progress and its applications, life, non-discrimination, equality, the prohibition against torture, privacy, access to information, and the freedoms of association, assembly and movement. Further, the Committee interpreted the right to health as an inclusive right extending not only to timely and appropriate health care but also to the underlying determinants of health, such as access to safe and potable water and adequate sanitation, an adequate supply of safe food, nutrition and housing, healthy occupational and environmental conditions, and access to health-related education and information, including on sexual and reproductive health. The General Comment sets out four criteria by which to evaluate the right to health:

(a) *Availability.* Functioning public health and health-care facilities, goods and services, as well as programmes, have to be available in sufficient quantity.

(b) *Accessibility.* Health facilities, goods and services have to be accessible to everyone without discrimination, within the jurisdiction of the State party. Accessibility has four overlapping dimensions:

- Non-discrimination;
- Physical accessibility;
- Economic accessibility (affordability);
- Information accessibility.

(c) *Acceptability.* All health facilities, goods and services must be respectful of medical ethics and culturally appropriate, sensitive to gender and life-cycle requirements, as well as being designed to respect confidentiality and improve the health status of those concerned.

(d) *Quality.* Health facilities, goods and services must be scientifically and medically appropriate and of good quality.

Discrimination in Health Care

Q.5 How does the principle of freedom from discrimination relate to health?

Vulnerable and marginalized groups in societies tend to bear an undue proportion of health problems. Overt or implicit discrimination violates a fundamental human rights principle and often lies at the root of poor health status. In practice, discrimination can manifest itself in inadequately targeted health programmes and restricted access to health services.

The prohibition of discrimination does not mean that differences should not be acknowledged, only that different treatment—and the failure to treat equal cases equally—must be based on objective and reasonable criteria intended to rectify imbalances within a society. In relation to health and health care the grounds for non-discrimination have

The Deadly Effects of Unaffordable Insurance

Estimated excess deaths among uninsured adults 25–64 for 2000

Age	U.S. Population 2000 (millions)	Uninsured Population 2000 (millions)	Total Deaths Estimated for 2000 Population	Uninsured Excess Deaths Estimated for 2000 Population
25–34	37,440	7,926	40,548	1,930
35–44	44,780	6,938	89,202	3,431
45–54	38,040	4,571	162,545	4,734
55–64	23,784	3,248	243,049	8,219
Total	144,044	22,683	535,344	18,314

Institute of Medicine, *Care Without Coverage: Too Little, Too Late*, 2002.

evolved and can now be summarized as proscribing any discrimination in access to health care and the underlying determinants of health, as well as to means and entitlements for their procurement, on the grounds of race, colour, sex, language, religion, political or other opinion, national or social origin, property, birth, physical or mental disability, health status (including HIV/AIDS), sexual orientation, civil, political, social or other status, which has the intention or effect of nullifying or impairing the equal enjoyment or exercise of the right to health. . . .

Connecting Health and Human Rights

Q.6 What is meant by a rights-based approach to health?
    A rights-based approach to health refers to the processes of:
    • *Using human rights as a framework for health development.*
    • *Assessing and addressing the human rights implications of any health policy, programme or legislation.*
    • *Making human rights an integral dimension of the design, implementation, monitoring and evaluation of health-related policies and programmes in all spheres, including political, economic and social.*
    Substantive elements to apply, within these processes, could be as follows:
    • Safeguarding *human dignity.*
    • Paying attention to those population groups considered most vulnerable in society.
    • In other words, recognizing and acting upon the charac-

teristics of those affected by health policies, programmes and strategies—children (girls and boys), adolescents, women, and men; indigenous and tribal populations; national, ethnic, religious and linguistic minorities; internally displaced persons; refugees; immigrants and migrants; the elderly; persons with disabilities; prisoners; economically disadvantaged or otherwise marginalized and/or vulnerable groups.

• Ensuring health systems are made *accessible* to all, especially the most vulnerable or marginalized sections of the population, in law and in fact, without discrimination on any of the prohibited grounds.

• Using a *gender* perspective, recognizing that both biological and sociocultural factors play a significant role in influencing the health of men and women, and that policies and programmes must consciously set out to address these differences.

• Ensuring *equality and freedom from discrimination*, advertent or inadvertent, in the way health programmes are designed or implemented.

• *Disaggregating* health data to detect underlying discrimination.

• Ensuring free, meaningful, and effective *participation* of beneficiaries of health development policies or programmes in decision-making processes which affect them.

• Promoting and protecting the *right to education* and the right to seek, receive and impart *information* and ideas concerning health issues. However, the right to information should not impair the right to *privacy*, which means that personal health data should be treated with confidentiality.

• Only limiting the exercise or enjoyment of a right by a health policy or programme as a last resort, and only considering this legitimate if each of the provisions reflected in *the Siracusa principles* is met. [The principles stipulate that any limitations must be "in response to a pressing public need."]

• Juxtaposing the human rights implications of any health legislation, policy or programme with the desired public health objectives and ensuring the *optimal balance* between good public health outcomes and the promotion and protection of human rights.

• Making *explicit linkages to international human rights*

norms and standards to highlight how human rights apply and relate to a health policy, programme or legislation.

• Making the attainment of the *right to the highest attainable standard of health* the explicit ultimate aim of activities, which have as their objective the enhancement of health.

• Articulating the concrete government *obligations* to respect, protect and fulfil human rights.

• Identifying *benchmarks and indicators* to ensure monitoring of the progressive realization of rights in the field of health.

• Increasing *transparency* in, and *accountability* for, health as a key consideration at all stages of programme development.

• Incorporating *safeguards* to protect against majoritarian threats upon minorities, migrants and other domestically "unpopular" groups, in order to address power imbalances. For example, by incorporating redress mechanisms in case of impingements on health-related rights. . . .

A Standard for Evaluation

Q.7 How can human rights support work to strengthen health systems?

Human rights provide a standard against which to evaluate existing health policies and programmes, including highlighting the differential treatment of individual groups of people in, for example, manifestations, frequency and severity of disease, and governmental responses to it. Human rights norms and standards also form a strong basis for health systems to prioritize the health needs of vulnerable and marginalized population groups. Human rights moves beyond averages and focuses attention on those population groups in society which are considered most vulnerable (e.g. indigenous and tribal populations; refugees and migrants; ethnic, religious, national and racial minorities), as well as putting forward specific human rights which may help guide health policy, programming, and health system processes (e.g. the right of those potentially affected by health policies, strategies and standards to participate in the process in which decisions affecting their health are made).

"It is problematic to consider healthcare as a 'right.'"

Health Care Is Not a Human Right

Richard D. Lamm

Although basic health care should be provided to all U.S. citizens, it must not be considered a human right, Richard D. Lamm argues in the following viewpoint. According to Lamm, rights are an ultimate value whose meaning is diluted if the label is ascribed to everything that is considered good and necessary in a just society. He asserts that the United States has limited resources that can be allocated to health care and that some restrictions are therefore inevitable, even if it means that certain medical treatments will not be available to all patients. Lamm is the former governor of Colorado and the director of the Center for Public Policy and Contemporary Issues at the University of Denver.

As you read, consider the following questions:
1. According to Lamm, third-party payers cover what fraction of hospital costs?
2. What are some of the methods by which governments ration health care, as stated by the author?
3. In Lamm's opinion, what have been the consequences of America's failure to discuss the problem of allocating resources toward health care?

Richard D. Lamm, "The Case Against Making Healthcare a 'Right,'" *Human Rights*, vol. 25, Fall 1998, pp. 8–11. Copyright © 1998 by the American Bar Association. Reproduced by permission.

All of the world's nations face a dual challenge in health-care—to expand basic healthcare to the medically indigent, yet to set limits on what benefits are to be subsidized by public policy. The latter task, setting limits, is an even harder challenge than the former because of the endless cures and treatments that technologically advanced societies can now provide to their aging populations. Nine-tenths of hospital costs and two-thirds of physicians' fees in the United States are paid by third-party payers. Whether government or private insurers, whoever allocates these dollars will have to set priorities on how to maximize health status within those limited resources. Which benefits do we pay for, and which ones don't we pay for? Every year there will be a different answer as technology and science enlarges our options. Guido Calabrisi, speaking generally of these dilemmas, says in his book, *Tragic Choices*:

> It is a dramatically different world than we have comfortably come to know. It will intrude upon values that society has come to think of as fundamental, of benefits that constituencies have come to think of as their right, and redefine as luxuries some things that people have come to see as necessities. We must attempt to make these choices in ways that do as little violence as possible to our moral and social traditions.

Resources Are Not Unlimited

We are embarking upon a new world of public policy choice. Our healthcare system and all its culture and ethics have developed under the assumption of unlimited resources. In thirty years, America's healthcare spending has gone from 4 percent of gross domestic product (GDP) to 14 percent of GDP at a growth rate two and a half times the rate of inflation. Our national health bill is now over one trillion dollars a year, by far the largest percentage and amount of resources in the health sector in the world. These statistics have allowed us to erroneously believe that we can meet all reasonable needs for all Americans.

Increasingly, we are recognizing that this is not the case. As health economist [Victor Fuchs] said so well, paraphrasing Winston Churchill ". . . a nation can provide all of its people with some of the care that might do them some good; it can provide some of its people with all the care that might do them some good; but it cannot provide all of its people with all of the care that might do them some good."

I applaud the goal of providing healthcare to all members of society. I have been fighting all my political life to cover the medically indigent with basic healthcare. However, in so doing, I have never argued that healthcare is a "right" or "human right." To make such an argument would be a public policy mistake.

Diluting the Meaning of "Rights"

"Rights" are defined and interpreted by the judicial system. A "right" trumps all other categories of social spending. It is the language of courts developed in an adversarial process. There is a Gresham's Law to language where we dilute or diminish the meaning of important words by overuse and overextension. I suggest that the word "rights" is one such word, desperately important but prone to overuse. If we are to successfully change public policy, we must take great care in our use of language and strategy. A just society has many "needs" that cannot and should not be reduced to "rights." "Rights" are ultimate values that a society must protect at all costs. They are our society's ultimate "Thou shalt nots."

It is problematic to consider healthcare as a "right." If everything is a right arguably, nothing is a right. We can easily dilute the important meaning of this word by claiming idealistically that all good things are "rights." It is a good-hearted mistake, but a mistake nonetheless. Even if it could be achieved, it would be counterproductive to the overall welfare of society.

Rights are an ineffective way of determining *who* or *what* is covered. The world of public policy is the world of choices, priorities, and tradeoffs. An institution must weigh total social need and cannot allow one social good to crowd out all others. As [Christopher Robbin] put it: "How can a state that lacks the resources to provide everyone who needs it with . . . renal dialysis, or a heart transplant, claim to be giving full effect to the right to health services? With the public's seemingly unending need for healthcare, how can any state reasonably recognize a universal right to services? Such acts of recognition would mean signing a blank check;

it would ruin the national economy."

Comparisons cannot be made between the many social goods a society must allocate using its legal system. Allocating finite resources over infinite needs is not advanced by the language of rights nor the province of courts. The judicial system is too blunt an instrument to weigh and balance either within the healthcare system or among total social needs.

Thus, public policy in most areas cannot be built around rights. Rights are adversarial and individual, where health policy has to balance both *who is covered* and *what is covered* for all citizens. It has to say both "yes" and "no." What is necessary is that we expand the moral vision of the legislative process. A caring government, not the judiciary, has a duty to the medically indigent. As Oregon Governor John Kitzhaber said: "The legislature is clearly accountable *not just* for what is funded in the healthcare budget, but also for what is *not* funded. Accountability is inescapable, a major departure from the current system."

We can and should provide basic healthcare to all citizens, but this should be done through the legislature, not the courts, and it should be accomplished as a matter of good social policy, not by playing the trump of rights.

A Balanced Approach

Public policy is filled with unmet needs. The moral agony of being a public servant is that there are so many important and worthy needs and goals and that it is not possible to satisfy them all. It is painful to balance and tradeoff between such valuable goals.

Every country in the world allocates limited resources among multiple needs. If government plays any role in healthcare, it has to prioritize needs. The method varies (some ration by price, some by queuing, some overtly by not making certain procedures available, and limiting procedures for people over certain ages), but all set limits. We are fooling ourselves when we do not admit that we too set limits. We, in fact, limit healthcare in one of the cruelest ways that any nation can do so—by simply leaving people out of the system. As one expert put it: rationing . . . is an integral component of our healthcare system, although we euphemistically call it by other names, for example, cost-sharing, preexisting condition limitations, or simply "uncovered" services. In many respects, there is little difference between these mechanisms and the existing policies in other countries that are openly acknowledged to ration care. It is not a question of whether rationing exists, but of what form it takes.

We can provide compassionate and comprehensive healthcare to all our citizens, but we cannot give everything. We must distinguish the many things that we do in modern medicine from what we *ought* to do with our limited resources.

Asay. © 1999 by Creators Syndicate, Inc. Reprinted with permission.

In a world of limited resources, we cannot say "yes" unless we say "no." We cannot explore the best use of our resources, the so-called "opportunity costs" of each dollar, unless we set priorities on what we can afford. We must start a community dialogue about how to put our healthcare dollars to the highest and best use. It is an inevitable discussion and we ought to make a virtue out of necessity.

The exciting challenge of healthcare reform is that many

thoughtful people believe we can give more health to more people for less money once we start to recognize that rationing is inevitable. [According to Brach Brody:]

As our population ages and as our abilities to provide good but expensive medical care increase, we will be facing a crisis in the growth of healthcare expenditure that neither physician, regulation, nor traditional market mechanisms were designed to confront. They were designed to provide alternative and acceptable ways of eliminating wasteful expenditures. It is easy to form a social consensus against waste. The only issue we have to face in fighting waste is the mixture of regulation and market mechanisms that best does the job and satisfies our other values. It is much harder to form a social consensus about which forms of useful healthcare should be denied to which recipients and it is therefore difficult to see how we can use either traditional approach in dealing with the real emerging crisis in the growth of healthcare expenditures.

This means we are going to have to spend as much time setting limits in healthcare as we expend expanding the coverage of healthcare. The price of a compassionate healthcare system is a restricted healthcare system. American medicine believes its duty is to deliver all of the healthcare that is "beneficial" to all patients—even marginally "beneficial." Thus, we have essentially invented a system without brakes—a system whose yardstick (i.e., a determination of what is "beneficial") is bound to bankrupt us. There is literally no end to "beneficial" medicine. There are so many things that we can do at the margin that are awesomely expensive, but essentially do not begin to meet any kind of test of cost-effectiveness in a society that has a variety of other unfilled social demands. We must put some public policy limits on the limitless concept of "beneficial."

A French study once gauged what it would cost to give all the healthcare that is "beneficial" to each citizen. The study found that it would cost five and one half times the French gross national product. Evidence from other societies suggests that all have found a way to limit the concept of "beneficial."

I believe the sum total of all "beneficial" medicine, as now defined, would be impossible to fund. More importantly, it would give us an unethical healthcare structure—unethical because it dramatically overspends on some patients, while other important social goals go unmet. The language of "rights" is not useful in correcting this imbalance that needs maximum flexibility.

The Views of Other Nations

One inevitable result of the healthcare dialogue in other countries is that the focus shifts from the individual to the larger question of: How do you buy health for society? These nations have come to the common sense conclusion that public policy ought to maximize a nation's *health*, not healthcare.

Clearly, public funds should be spent in a way that will maximize their effectiveness. We cannot build a healthcare system (particularly a publicly funded one) one patient at a time. Inevitably, nations must start to ask: What policies buy the most health for the most people?

Canada, for instance, commissioned a study, "The Determinants of Health," that examined which policies brought the most health for Canada. The study arose out of a dilemma similar to one now occurring in the United States. The study found that Canadians were spending too much on healthcare and not enough on other health-enhancing activities.

Many people have pointed out that spending money on the healthcare system was not the best way to a healthy society. The study urged Canadians to expand their concept of health far beyond medical care and to "adopt a new framework for understanding health. The challenge of the future lies in using this knowledge to develop effective policies that will ensure a healthy and prosperous society."

A similar dialogue is going on all over the developed world. How does a society produce health? Increasingly, the answer is that the healthcare system is only a small part of the solution. Nations must start to focus on health, not healthcare.

Achieving a healthy society may thus involve saying no to certain aspects of healthcare. Health may be best achieved in other areas of social policy. Archie Cochrane, the famous British physician, recognized this when in 1972, he refused to support more resources to Britain's National Health Services (NHS) observing there was more health in other areas of social policy. "I have no intention of joining the clamor for far more money for the NHS. If more money becomes available for the welfare services, I think an increase in old-age pensions should have priority."

We have not had this dialogue in the United States. We've never asked: How do we spend our resources to achieve the most health? The results of this failure are tragic: too much spent on allopathic medicine—too little spent on public health; and too many specialists—too few primary physicians. We need a larger vision of health than the leaders of healthcare have given us—and to achieve that we need a broader conversation removed from talk of a "right to healthcare."

The Price of Modern Medicine

It is wonderful rhetoric to claim on the political stump that all citizens ought to have a "right to healthcare." But it is not good public policy. Medical policy and ethics focus mainly on the individual, and urge—under the pain of a lawsuit—to do everything that is "beneficial" or will "add value" to that patient. This standard soon runs into the law of diminishing returns and simultaneously distributes limited resources ineffectively. The price of modern medicine is to decide what to cover among the smorgasbord of treatments available.

The healthcare system can no more afford to do everything "beneficial" for every patient than the education system can do everything "beneficial" for every student, nor the police department do everything "beneficial" for every citizen, nor every parent do everything "beneficial" for their children. We are judging much of what we do and expect in health from an unsustainable yardstick.

No matter how we organize and no matter how we fund healthcare, we will find our medical miracles have outpaced our ability to pay. It is hard to change our thinking after years of blank check medicine—but necessary. As David Eddy said, "We will need to accept, once and for all, that resources are limited. It is the limitation on resources that both necessitates and justifies the strategy of getting more for less." This is painful, but unavoidable. We are inventing the unaffordable and spending the unsustainable. We need to focus limited resources on where they will buy the most health for society.

A decent and just society is a structure with many important pillars. Healthcare is one of those pillars but so is education, justice, welfare, decent infrastructure, and liveable environment. My generation has been mesmerized by the concept of rights because the concept was so useful in expanding freedom and justice. But "rights" are not a universal tool applicable to every social need.

"A key consequence of the proliferation of human rights is the deterioration of personal responsibility."

Defining Human Rights Too Broadly Can Destroy Nations

John A. Gentry

In the following viewpoint, John A. Gentry argues that the overly broad definition of human rights adopted in the United States has led to numerous problems. In his opinion, Americans wrongly believe they are entitled to complete economic security and protection against all kinds of discrimination. Gentry claims that this sense of entitlement has led to a decline in personal responsibility and the privileging of some groups over others, which threatens national cohesion. Gentry is a former CIA analyst who researches and writes on defense and national security.

As you read, consider the following questions:
1. In Gentry's opinion, when did the creation of rights in the United States begin to accelerate?
2. How do excessive human rights destroy nationhood, according to the author?
3. Why does the former prime minister of Singapore believe that the spread of human rights in the United States is dysfunctional?

John A. Gentry, "The Cancer of Human Rights," *Washington Quarterly*, vol. 22, Autumn 1999, pp. 95–101.

The development of a broad variety of rights is a prominent feature of social and political life in the late second millennium. The establishment of political rights in the U.S. Constitution and its first ten amendments were a radical break from the political norms of the late eighteenth century. The growth and spread of these rights, and the philosophy they embodied, had a profound influence on the development of the United States and on ideas throughout the world.

The notion that good countries grant specific rights to their citizens has evolved to the point that many persons believe that innate "human rights" belong to all people—and that these rights transcend and subordinate national governments and social norms. Governments exist to provide resources to actualize the promises of human rights. Not surprisingly, ostensibly universal rights look much like those that developed in North America and Europe.

Going Beyond Elemental Rights

Elemental political rights, such as freedoms of speech and religion of the sort embodied in the U.S. Constitution, are political forces that largely define democratic societies. They allow much opportunity for individual growth and personal freedom. Many persons thus see such rights as powerful forces for good. I will not argue differently.

The expansion of rights from beyond elemental guarantees of personal opportunity and protections from state tyranny to much more numerous, tailored rights that guarantee results in narrow aspects of life, however, is causing problems. Rights are costly and dangerous when they disrupt traditional and effective organizational structures, contradict religious and secular moral values, and unbalance previously functional social systems. They render ineffective or incompetent the foreign policies of states led or strongly influenced by strong human-rights adherents. They lead to and prolong conflicts rather than resolve them. The unbridled growth of human rights accentuates differences among persons and groups, threatens internal order and social cohesion, and transforms nations into mere states. In the worst cases the uncontrolled growth of rights, like cancer cells, can kill the hosts that nurture them—and thereby kill themselves.

The United States most clearly reflects an advanced development of human rights, both domestically and in foreign policies, but it is not unique. Other countries and a powerful international group of human rights advocates—in and out of national governments—have altered the conduct of international affairs.

The Entitlement Ethic

The proliferation of rights in the United States is pandemic. Once restricted to the major rights embodied in the Constitution, the legal, regulatory, cultural, and commercial rights of residents of the United States are massive and growing. Creation of rights has accelerated since the 1960s, when Great Society social programs [President Lyndon B. Johnson's efforts to end poverty] were based in part on rights-based arguments. These benefits are part of the entitlement structure of the U.S. federal government and its mandates on state and local governments. This phenomenon helped generate what is known as an entitlement ethic—the notion that receipt of government services and cash is a right. This view, evident in many ways, permeates U.S. society.

The creation of rights has spread from fundamental political guarantees to economic safety nets, consumption-support programs, government administrative procedures, and trivial matters of personal convenience. The creation of rights has shifted toward narrow functional issues and the assurance of outcomes rather than processes, opportunities, and protections. New legislative, administrative, and court-ordered rights in recent years gave handicapped persons rights to access to public transportation and buildings, often at substantial private and public financial cost. Partners of homosexuals won rights to medical insurance coverage similar to legally married persons in some jurisdictions. The U.S. Congress embodied a second "taxpayer bill of rights" in legislation in 1998 to modestly reform the Internal Revenue Service. Many people argue that respect is an entitlement right, not something that is earned. Commercial firms see the appeal of rights and offer variations of "consumers' rights." The list is long.

The establishment of rights creates high standards for acceptable performance that society and government cannot achieve. Because rights as entitlements are not things to be earned or purchased at market prices, people demand immediate consumption of lots of them. People expect the rights to meet absolute standards of quality and timeliness that usually are not attainable. Resources are scarce. Moreover, some rights grant persons changes in the behavior of people with whom they associate, even casually. As animals with limited intellectual capacities and abundant sociopolitical teachings or prejudices embodied in their cultures, people cannot and often do not want to perform to the standards of contemporary Western idealism.

The complex of alleged rights is internally inconsistent. So many rights exist that all U.S. citizens now are victims of discrimination—the failure of government or society to assure one or more explicit or perceived rights. The United States now has true equality of victimization. Further, the gap between slowly rising resources and more rapidly increasing demands to satisfy rights-rationalized agendas is growing. This amounts to a new variant of the "revolution of rising expectations" that originally referred to the political consequences of the slow realization of economic ambitions.

Damaging Nationhood

The proliferation of human rights is a boon for rights-oriented bureaucracies and trial lawyers, but it damages the social fabric that turns groups of people into communities and communities into a nation. Because the only asset any government ultimately has is its legitimacy, the cost of a government's inability to satisfy rights-based demands is overwhelming. That cost rises further when governments, and the political parties that seek to control them, favor some rights over competing claims to please political backers or to curry favor with voters.

Excessive human rights are anathema to nationhood because they denigrate the compromise, discipline, and sacrifice needed for collective work in pursuit of common goals in favor of the immediate gratification of individual desires. With personal desires enshrined as rights through justifications of ideology or theology, there is no need to share them or to compromise on their definition, cost, or speed of actualization. Rights are absolute by definition. With claims to rights clear, the shared community values and goals that helped bond society when rights were fewer and resource constraints more obvious are much less important. There is less need to work together and thus less of the glue of nationhood. Even when nationhood is diminished or destroyed, however, government structures remain to service the rights of individuals and small groups, including the employment rights of bureaucracies and unions built to provide services justified by rights.

Rights and Responsibilities

The right to be recognized as a person before the law implies the responsibility to obey the law—and to make both the laws and the legal system more just. Likewise, in the socioeconomic realm, the right to marry carries with it the responsibility to support the family unit, to educate one's children and to treat all family members with respect. The right to work cannot be divorced from the responsibility to perform one's duties to the best of one's ability. In the broadest sense, the notion of "universal" human rights implies a responsibility to humanity as a whole. This interplay between rights and responsibilities has, for nearly fifty years, been acknowledged in Article 29 of the Universal Declaration of Human Rights. . . . Human rights education should accordingly focus on developing an awareness of the connection between rights and responsibilities and of the personal responsibility we each have to safeguard the rights of our fellow human beings.

Bahá'í International Community, "The United Nations Decade for Human Rights Education," March 1996.

Although initially created as individual properties, human rights are easily aggregated to become collective assets of groups of similar individuals. The logical step is small, but the consequences of this action are sometimes very large because group rights are different from and greater than the sum of rights of individuals. Just as individuals have alleged rights of opportunity and sometimes results, activists often claim that the collective ambitions of groups deserve actualization as rights. The variously defined performances of groups in society—be they consumption levels, unemployment rates, or inmate populations—must in aggregate be at least equal to that of other groups without consideration of troublesome distractions such as historical and cultural factors, labor force participation rates, and work ethics. As in [humorist Garrison Keillor's] Lake Wobegone, everyone must be at least average. Subpar performance by any of a host of measures is allegedly evidence of discrimination.

As for individuals, the rights of groups allegedly are immutable and merit immediate gratification. Because they too are absolute, there is no appropriate compromise among the demands for group rights. The result is proliferation of strident social subgroups of special interests little inclined to work constructively with one another except for reasons of tactical expediency. The degeneration of U.S. society into narrow interest groups further diminishes the nationhood of the United States. Countless commentators have identified symptoms; single-issue groups constitute a growing share of politically active citizens, for example.

Political Instability

[Professor of international relations] Samuel Huntington made the point differently by observing that, in the name of multiculturalism, powerful forces in the United States are accentuating the differences among U.S. residents and encouraging their preservation. By so doing, these persons attack the identity of the United States as a member of Western civilization. Failure to assimilate immigrant groups risks transformation of the United States into what Huntington calls a cleft country, with potentially dire consequences for political stability. This amounts to an attack on the whole in the name of the perceived rights of groups that refuse to assimilate.

Countries that are not nations can survive a long time in the absence of a crisis. They are prone to fail in the face of external threat but may explode, however, if the crisis is internal. They are especially likely to fail if disparate groups, bolstered by the certainty that they hold rights to their goals, strive for self-gratification at the expense of other groups. If groups threaten the perceived vital interests of other groups, including perceived human rights, civil war may result. This happened in Bosnia in 1992 and in Kosovo in 1998. Although not an immediate threat, it could happen in California, too.

A United States that protects and advances under the rubric of rights the parochial interests of discrete but politically powerful groups, including bureaucratic constituencies, must damage the traditional freedoms of small groups and individuals, either absolutely or by relative deprivation compared with favored groups. Disregard for, or subordination of, the rights of the politically weak generates substantial unhappiness among persons and groups personally aggrieved or disillusioned with the failure of the country to honor its promises. Antigovernment groups thus flourish in the late twentieth century in the United States. Timothy McVeigh swore allegiance to the United States as an U.S. Army soldier but became angry enough with its government to attack it physically in Oklahoma City in 1995.

Even in the absence of civil war, part of government in an age of human rights must become impersonal and disconnected from the lives of citizens, that is, the part that through taxation fills the economic trough that feeds people who are transformed from taxpayers to rights holders. Obtuse tax systems enable governments to accomplish this magic by separating the pleasures of receiving baskets of entitlements—and the benevolence of politicians for providing them—from the magnitude and timing of the pain of taxation.

Lee Kuan Yew, prime minister of Singapore from 1959 to 1990, and others have noted the deleterious effects of the proliferation of individual rights in the West in general and the United States in particular. Lee has noted that the proliferation of rights in the United States is dysfunctional because it places the freedom of individuals above the interests of society as a whole. This damages the coherence of society and eventually those same individual freedoms, broadly defined to include freedom of individual action and personal safety.

A Loss of Responsibility

A key consequence of the proliferation of human rights is the deterioration of personal responsibility. When the government guarantees rights, there is no need for personal responsibility in those aspects of life the rights cover. There is no personal responsibility to pay for rights that states exist to deliver. Thus the idea of a personal payment, denominated in money, time, or blood, for rights-based objectives is offensive. Virtually any price is too high, hence the need for an obtuse, federal fiscal policy. In a world dominated by human rights, humans should expect to get what they want without paying. Rights come without strings. Rights do not bear the symmetrical burdens of duty and responsibility that privileges carry. In a rights-based society, privileges have little value and compel correspondingly modest obligations.

Personal irresponsibility borne in part by the proliferation of human rights has spread to many aspects of life in the United States. The decay of national fiscal responsibility, interrupted temporarily in the late 1990s by a booming economy and a movement toward budget balance, is caused largely by demands on the resources of a distant impersonal state. Many people presume that this state has deep pockets filled with resources that are numerous and free. At the personal level, the penchant to satisfy desires immediately is a major cause of the long-term decline in personal savings at rates that long have been below other industrialized countries and that in late 1998 and 1999 was negative for the first time since the 1930s. Personal irresponsibility aided by lax bankruptcy laws surely is a major cause of the otherwise incongruous surge in personal bankruptcies during the boom years of the late 1990s.

The attitudes of U.S. citizens toward human rights and responsibilities have changed significantly in a relatively short time. Presidents and the citizenry have long felt that something special about the United States makes the advancement of good an ideal that the United States should pay to advance. President John Kennedy eloquently said in his inaugural address that his administration would not permit "the slow undoing of those human rights to which this nation has always been committed, and to which we are committed today at home and around the world. Let every nation know, whether it wishes us well or ill, that we shall pay any price, bear any burden, oppose any foe to assure the survival and success of liberty."

But in recent years, support for human rights has evolved toward carping. The United States has been little inclined to pay much of a tangible price for human rights, even for clear national interests.

| *"The human rights community's deadliest enemy is double standards."*

Human Rights Are Often Defined Inconsistently

William Ratliff

Human rights organizations such as Amnesty International and Asia Watch behave as though human rights abuses can occur only under right-wing dictators, William Ratliff contends in the following viewpoint. He maintains that this leftist definition of human rights leads activists to approve the arrest of human rights abusers on the right, such as former Chilean dictator Augusto Pinochet, while ignoring the brutal behavior of abusers on the left, such as Cuban leader Fidel Castro. According to Ratliff, the human rights community must break free of this double standard and seek justice for all people, regardless of their political views. Ratliff is a senior research fellow at the Hoover Institution, which seeks to improve the human condition and safeguard peace.

As you read, consider the following questions:

1. How does Ratliff believe that Baltasar Garzon could have demonstrated political balance after arresting Augusto Pinochet?
2. In the author's view, why is Rigoberta Menchu a "fraudulent spokeswoman" for indigenous people in Central America?
3. According to Ratliff, what were some of the crimes perpetrated by the Japanese during World War II?

U. N. Secretary-General Kofi Annan hailed the 50th anniversary of the United Nations' "Universal Declaration of Human Rights" on [December 10, 1998,] as "a day for celebration, a day for remembrance, and a day for commitment."

It was all that, but it should also have been a day for profound self-examination. Many in the international "human rights" community have done much recently to discredit themselves and the cause.

Bias Is on the Rise

Developments include aggressive campaigns on behalf of victims of right-wing dictators only; more evidence on the tragic impact of the politicization of the Nobel Peace Prize; and continuing indifference to "burying" one of the 20th century's most heinous crimes against humanity.

It's the same question Bob Dylan asked long ago: "How many times can a man turn his head and pretend that he just doesn't see?" When the Cold War ended, political bias as the motivation for supporting human rights for some and not for others seemed to decline, though not everywhere—e.g., in Nicaragua, whose human rights defenders in the 1990s were systematically ignored. Balance seemed to be increasing until the Pinochet affair, which Amnesty International has called a "new era for human rights." New? More like a return to the old.

Irresponsible Actions

Whatever one thinks of the substance of Spanish magistrate Baltasar Garzon's case against former Chilean dictator Augusto Pinochet [during whose seventeen-year term three thousand people were murdered or mysteriously disappeared], his actions are as contemptuous of impartiality as they are irresponsible.

An impartial magistrate would have defused the inevitable explosive politics of arresting Pinochet by going as far as necessary to demonstrate political balance. Garzon could have simultaneously issued a warrant for the arrest of Fidel Castro. If Castro could not be picked up because he is still Cuba's leader, Garzon could have issued warrants for former

Sandinista President Daniel Ortega of Nicaragua and his thuggish interior minister, Tomas Borge.

Meanwhile, an investigation into Castro's crimes in Cuba and many countries abroad could have begun with the same international cooperation that rights advocates want given to the investigation of Pinochet.

Garzon's action was irresponsible because, as Amnesty International's U.S. Executive Director William Shulz says, this kind of prosecution is still "a very ad hoc procedure"—though Shulz endorses it. Indeed! Garzon has thrown an extremely complicated and controversial case in the lap of an international-justice system whose guidelines and instruments remain woefully inadequate for this job.

But, since rogues do such things by nature, the main problem is that Garzon's actions have been so uncritically supported by others. Amnesty International says justice for Pinochet "would send a clear message to the world's torturers and death squads that they cannot commit their crimes with impunity." But while Amnesty International talks of making tyrants tremble, events suggest otherwise. Unless the rights community becomes much more politically balanced, it will never launch equally vigorous campaigns to get justice for victims of the Castros and Borges—and those old leftists know it. In effect, Garzon has said, "I've got my demon, you go get yours if you can"—which, if Pinochet is extradited, many others will try to do. That is a prescription for chaos.

The Rigoberta Menchu Controversy

Another human rights personality from the Cold War is in the news again: Rigoberta Menchu, winner of the 1992 Nobel Peace Prize. David Stoll has published "Rigoberta Menchu and the Story of All Poor Guatemalans," which shows that her 1983 "autobiography" that led to the Nobel Prize is less Menchu's life and more a "morality play"—an often-misleading one at that.

Menchu got the award for political reasons, as is common with peace prizes. The Nobel Committee sought to recognize indigenous peoples on the 500th anniversary of the "discovery" of America and to condemn repression in Guatemala—

matters of merit—but it chose the wrong recipient and created a fraudulent spokeswoman for the indigenous peoples of the Americas.

Not Non-Political

All [human-rights] groups primly maintain that they are non-political. Yet their agenda is often indistinguishable from that of left-liberals. Amnesty issues reports on racial disparities in imprisonment in the United States—another alleged human-rights abuse; it is rarely mentioned that racial disparities in crime rates might be relevant to the situation. Amnesty wants Leonard Peltier, who was convicted of killing two FBI agents but is also a cause celebre of the Left, released.

Ramesh Ponnuru, *National Review*, April 8, 2002.

Menchu's passion was Marxist revolution, not human rights. In fact, the prize glorified a woman who militantly supported brutal Sandinista repression of the Miskito Indians and others in Nicaragua in the early 1980s and brought grief to the Indians in her own country. Stoll shows how she was used by outsiders "to justify continuing a war (in Guatemala) at the expense of the peasants who did not support it"—with untold and senseless casualties. Menchu promoted her political passion effectively because, like the Spanish rogue magistrate, she (and her supporters) knew how to tell politicized urban audiences abroad what they wanted to hear in order to pursue their own objectives— which were often hers as well, but not those of most indigenous peoples.

[In December 1998] the founder of the Guerrilla Army of the Poor, which Menchu supported, asked the Guatemalan people to forgive him for his past. Menchu—a celebrated guest of honor at a 50th-anniversary celebration in Paris, which Amnesty International called its "first ever world summit of human rights defenders"—however, simply says all who challenge her past are "racists."

Indifference to Japanese Atrocities

The chief case of indifference by human rights groups relates to Japan's crimes in China during World War II. There is no statute of limitations on Nazi crimes in Europe, but what of the concurrent and often equal Japanese atrocities in China?

These latter were of such a scale and ferocity as to make all the repression by all Latin American dictators of the 20th century combined seem almost mild by comparison.

Chinese President Jiang Zemin pressed for an apology when he went to Japan in November [1998], but he did not follow Garzon's lead and demand the extradition of presumed war criminals for trial. All he wanted was an apology, along the lines of the one Tokyo had made to Korea.

One might suppose that rights advocates who are surpassingly concerned about 3,000 Chileans a quarter-century ago would have equal concern for Chinese the Japanese raped, mutilated and/or conducted grotesque medical experiments on. Between 75,000 and 300,000 were tortured and killed over several months in the city of Nanjing alone, while tens of millions died during Japan's unprovoked 14-year invasion and occupation.

But when Japan refused to give the apology, there was no international protest or pressure. With its absolute silence—not even a press release from Amnesty International or Asia Watch—the rights community spoke loudly on these crimes against Chinese: "They're not important like Nazi crimes! Forget them, as we have!"

Human Rights Groups Must Seek the Truth

The human rights community's deadliest enemy is double standards. Now that the celebrations have passed, advocates should analyze what is happening and act on the understanding that the most important commodity they have is the truth. It must be an impartial truth—one that seeks justice even for Chinese, anti-Castro Cubans, former Contras and indigenous peoples who don't like Marxist guerrillas. Tragically, many in the rights community fail to recognize or admit their bias. Thus it continues, reducing the credibility and impact of rights groups even where they do excellent work, and impeding moves to create fair, workable international enforcement standards and mechanisms.

The bias is all the more frustrating and inexcusable because it could so easily be overcome—if only the truth and impartiality that rights groups claim as their guiding principles were adhered to consistently.

Periodical Bibliography

The following articles have been selected to supplement the diverse views presented in this chapter.

Alison Barnes and
Michael McChrystal
"The Various Human Rights in Healthcare," *Human Rights*, Fall 1998.

Barbara Crossette
"Testing the Limits of Tolerance as Cultures Mix," *New York Times*, March 6, 1999.

John Fonte
"The Progressive Challenge to American Democracy," *American Outlook*, Spring 2000.

Mary Ann Glendon
and Elliott Abrams
"Reflections on the UDHR," *First Things*, April 1998.

Thomas Hammarberg
"Not by Bread Alone . . . But Not Without Bread Either," *UN Chronicle*, Winter 1998.

Uwe-Jens Heuer and
Gregor Schirmer,
trans. Anita Mage
"Human Rights Imperialism," *Monthly Review*, March 1998.

Elizabeth Khaxas
"Sexual Rights Are Human Rights," *Siecus Report*, June/July 2001.

Shulamith Koenig
et al.
"Economic, Social, and Cultural Rights: Questions and Answers," *The Fourth R*, Spring 1998.

Graça Machel
"The Universal Declaration of Human Rights: From Words to Deeds," *Christian Social Action*, December 1998.

David R. Penna and
Patricia J. Campbell
"Human Rights and Culture: Beyond Universality and Relativism," *Third World Quarterly*, March 1998.

Ramesh Ponnuru
"Watching the Watchmen," *National Review*, April 8, 2002.

Henry Rosemont Jr.
"Reflections on Human Rights Conflicts," *Resist*, November 1998.

Amartya Sen
"Universal Truths," *Harvard International Review*, Summer 1998.

Christine Stolba
"The Beijing Brigade," *Women's Quarterly*, Winter 2000.

Shashi Tharoor
"Are Human Rights Universal?" *World Policy Journal*, Winter 1999–2000.

CHAPTER 2

What Is the State of Human Rights?

Chapter Preface

Religious persecution is one of the most common of human rights violations. In ancient Rome, Christians were thrown to the lions; during the Inquisition, Jews and Muslims faced forced conversions, expulsion, torture, and executions. While the perpetrators and methods might have changed, religious persecution remains a serious problem throughout the world. According to the U.S. State Department's Annual Report on International Religious Freedom, three of the worst modern-day offenders are China, Sudan, and Saudi Arabia.

The Chinese government recognizes five religions: Buddhism, Taoism, Islam, Catholicism, and Protestantism. However, adherents of those faiths are not guaranteed complete freedom of worship. According to Nina Shea, a human-rights lawyer and director for the Center for Religious Freedom at Freedom House, "All religious believers must worship within churches sanctioned and controlled by the government. Christians, Tibetan Buddhists, and Muslims who persist in praying independently are sent to labor camp, imprisoned, or heavily fined." Catholics and Protestants, in particular, have suffered, with hundreds of Chinese Christian leaders imprisoned and tortured, sometimes fatally. Tibetan Buddhist monks have been similarly mistreated.

In China, religious persecution is committed at the behest of an ostensibly nonreligious Communist government. The human rights abuses in Sudan and Saudi Arabia are examples of what can happen when a nation is under the control of a militant religious government. Paul Marshall, a senior fellow at the Center for Religious Freedom, writes, "In Sudan the real power is Hassan Turabi, leader of the National Islamic Front. The western-educated Turabi is leading a program of Islamization through genocide." The Sudanese government has overseen the slaughter of 1.5 million Christians, animists, and other non-Muslims. Muslims who convert to other religions are executed. Non-Muslims in Sudan who are spared the death penalty have endured a number of other indignities, including kidnapping and forced conversion, enslavement, imprisonment, and torture.

The situation in Saudi Arabia is similar. Shea writes: "In its role as the keeper of global Islam, the Saudi Arabian government does not tolerate any practice of religion other than Islam—either by its own citizens or by foreigners." The government relies on religious police, known as *muttawa*, to find evidence of illegal worship. No non-Muslim places of worship can be built, and people found practicing Christianity have been imprisoned and even executed. As in Sudan, any Muslim who attempts to leave the faith runs the risk of execution.

China, Sudan, and Saudi Arabia are not the only nations guilty of human rights abuses, nor is religious persecution the only serious human rights problem in the modern world. In the following chapter, the authors consider the state of human rights. Unfortunately, persecution such as that which took place in ancient Rome and during the Inquisition still occurs in some regions of the world.

*"Even if the detainees were not [prisoners
of war], they remain human beings with
human rights."*

The United States Has Violated the Geneva Convention in Its Treatment of Terrorist Suspects

Michael Byers

Following the September 11, 2001, terrorist attacks on
America, the United States sent troops to Afghanistan to
battle the ruling Taliban and the al-Qaeda terrorist network
deemed responsible for the attacks. Captured Taliban and al-
Qaeda fighters were transported to the U.S. military outpost
at Guantánamo Bay in Cuba. In the following viewpoint,
Michael Byers asserts that the United States has violated international human rights agreements in its treatment of the
detainees. According to Byers, the United States has been
inhumane and degrading toward the detainees by forcibly
sedating them and shaving off their beards, among other human rights violations. Byers is a professor of international
law at Duke University.

As you read, consider the following questions:
1. According to Byers, why do the detainees at Guantánamo
   Bay have no rights under the U.S. Constitution?
2. In the author's opinion, when is it most important for
   human rights to be applied?
3. What has the widespread sympathy for the United States
   in the wake of the September 11, 2001, attacks enabled
   the nation to do, according to the author?

Michael Byers, "U.S. Doesn't Have a Right to Decide Who Is or Isn't a POW,"
Guardian, January 14, 2002. Copyright © 2002 by Guardian Newspapers
Limited. Reproduced by permission of the author.

W ould you want your life to be in the hands of U.S. secretary of defence Donald Rumsfeld? Hundreds of captured Taliban and al-Qaida fighters don't have a choice.[1] Chained, manacled, hooded, even sedated, their beards shorn off against their will, they are being flown around the world to Guantanamo Bay, a century-old military outpost seized during the Spanish-American war and subsequently leased from Cuba by the U.S. There, they are being kept in tiny chain-link outdoor cages, without mosquito repellent, where (their captors assure us) they are likely to be rained upon.

Since Guantanamo Bay is technically foreign territory, the detainees have no rights under the U.S. constitution and cannot appeal to U.S. federal courts. Any rights they might have under international law have been firmly denied. According to Rumsfeld, the detainees "will be handled not as prisoners of war, because they are not, but as unlawful combatants".

Determining the Status of Detainees

This unilateral determination of the detainees' status is highly convenient, since the 1949 Geneva convention on the treatment of prisoners of war (POWs) stipulates that POWs can only be tried by "the same courts according to the same procedure as in the case of members of the armed forces of the detaining power". The Pentagon clearly intends to prosecute at least some of the detainees in special military commissions having looser rules of evidence and a lower burden of proof than regular military or civilian courts. This will help to protect classified information, but also substantially increase the likelihood of convictions. The rules of evidence and procedure for the military commissions will be issued later [in January 2002] by none other than Donald Rumsfeld.

The Geneva convention also makes it clear that it isn't for Rumsfeld to decide whether the detainees are ordinary criminal suspects rather than POWs. Anyone detained in the course of an armed conflict is presumed to be a POW until a competent court or tribunal determines otherwise. The record shows that those who negotiated the convention were

---

1. The Taliban was the government in Afghanistan at the time of the September 2001 terrorist attacks; al-Qaeda is the terrorist network responsible for the attacks.

intent on making it impossible for the determination to be made by any single person.

Once in front of a court or tribunal, the Pentagon might argue that the Taliban were not the government of Afghanistan and that their armed forces were not the armed forces of a party to the convention. The problem here is that the convention is widely regarded as an accurate statement of customary international law, unwritten rules binding on all. Even if the Taliban were not formally a party to the convention, both they and the U.S. would still have to comply.

The Pentagon might also argue that al-Qaida members were not part of the Taliban's regular armed forces. Traditionally, irregulars could only benefit from POW status if they wore identifiable insignia, which al-Qaida members seem not to have done. But the removal of the Taliban regime was justified on the basis that al-Qaida and the Taliban were inextricably linked, a justification that weakens the claim that the former are irregulars.

Questionable Treatment of Detainees

Moreover, the convention has to be interpreted in the context of modern international conflicts, which share many of the aspects of civil wars and tend not to involve professional soldiers on both sides. Since the convention is designed to protect persons, not states, the guiding principle has to be the furtherance of that protection. This principle is manifest in the presumption that every detainee is a POW until a competent court or tribunal determines otherwise.

This too is the position of the International Committee of the Red Cross, which plays a supervisory role over the convention. The Red Cross and Amnesty International have both expressed concerns over the treatment of the detainees. The authorities at Guantanamo Bay have prohibited journalists from filming the arrival of the detainees on the basis that the convention stipulates POWs "must at all times be protected against insults and public curiosity". The hypocrisy undermines the position on POW status: you can't have your cake and eat it.

Even if the detainees were not POWs, they remain human beings with human rights. Hooding, even temporarily, constitutes a violation of the 1984 convention against torture and cruel, inhuman or degrading treatment. Apart from causing unnecessary mental anguish, it prevents a detainee from identifying anyone causing them harm. Forcefully shaving off their beards constitutes a violation of the right to human dignity under the 1966 international covenant on

A Series of Violations

The USA has denied or threatens to deny internationally recognized rights of people taken into its custody in Afghanistan and elsewhere, including those transferred to Camp X-Ray in Guantánamo Bay. Among other things, Amnesty International is concerned that the US Government has:

• transferred and held people in conditions that may amount to cruel, inhuman or degrading treatment, and that violate other minimum standards relating to detention;

• refused to inform people in its custody of all their rights;

• refused to grant people in its custody access to legal counsel, including during questioning by US and other authorities;

• refused to grant people in its custody access to the courts to challenge the lawfulness of their detention;

• undermined the presumption of innocence through a pattern of public commentary on the presumed guilt of the people in its custody in Guantánamo Bay;

• failed to facilitate promptly communications with or grant access to family members;

• undermined due process and extradition protections in cases of people taken into custody outside Afghanistan and transferred to Guantánamo Bay;

• threatened to select foreign nationals for trial before military commissions, executive bodies lacking clear independence from the executive and with the power to hand down death sentences, and without the right of appeal to an independent and impartial court;

• raised the prospect of indefinite detention without charge or trial, or continued detention after acquittal, or repatriation that may threaten the principle of non-refoulement;

• failed to show that it has conducted an impartial and thorough investigation into allegations of human rights violations against Afghan villagers detained by US soldiers.

Amnesty International, "Memorandum to the U.S. Government on the Rights of People in U.S. Custody in Afghanistan and Guantánamo Bay," 2002.

civil and political rights. Forcefully sedating even one detainee for non-medical reasons violates international law. Although strict security arrangements are important in dealing with potentially dangerous individuals, none of these measures are necessary to achieving that goal. If human rights are worth anything, they have to apply when governments are most tempted to violate them.

There are many reasons why these and other violations are unacceptable. The rights of the detainees are our rights as well. Yet international law can be modified as a result of state behaviour. If we stand by while the rights of the detainees are undermined, we, as individuals, could lose.

Human Rights Must Be Upheld

British and American soldiers and aid workers operate around the world in conflict zones dominated by quasi-irregular forces. The violations in Guantanamo Bay will undermine the ability of our governments to ensure adequate treatment the next time our fellow citizens are captured and held. Respecting the presumption of POW status and upholding the human rights of detainees today will help to protect our people in future.

The U.S. has occupied much of the moral high ground since September 11, 2001, and benefited enormously from so doing. Widespread sympathy for the U.S. has made it much easier to freeze financial assets and secure the detention of suspects overseas, as well as secure intelligence sharing and military support. The sympathy has also bolstered efforts to win the hearts and minds of ordinary people in the Middle East, south Asia and elsewhere. That might just have prevented further terrorist attacks.

Ignoring even some of the rights of those detained in Guantanamo Bay squanders this intangible but invaluable asset, in return for nothing but the fleeting satisfaction of early revenge. The detainees should be accorded full treatment as POWs and, if not released in due course, tried before regular military or civilian courts—or even better, an ad hoc international tribunal. As the world watches, vengeance is ours. But so, too, are civilised standards of treatment and justice.

"Not only has al Qaeda not signed the Geneva Convention, al Qaeda and the Taliban aren't even governments."

The United States Has Not Violated the Geneva Convention in Its Treatment of Terrorist Suspects

Richard Lowry

In the following viewpoint, Richard Lowry asserts that the United States has not violated the Geneva Convention—an international agreement which established standards for the treatment of prisoners of war—in its handling of captive Taliban and al-Qaeda fighters. According to Lowry, these detainees, who were captured when the United States invaded Afghanistan following the September 11, 2001, terrorist attacks, are not legitimate prisoners of war. He argues that the Geneva Convention does not apply to the detainees held at Guantánamo Bay, Cuba, because neither the Taliban nor al-Qaeda are legitimate governments and thus are not entitled to the reciprocity of the Geneva Convention. Lowry is an editor at the *National Review*.

As you read, consider the following questions:
1. How does the Geneva Convention protect innocent civilians, as stated by Lowry?
2. According to Jeremy Rabkin, as cited by Lowry, what is at the heart of the Geneva Convention?
3. What is "the rules of proportionality," as defined by the author?

W hat is it that the [George W.] Bush administration's European critics like so much about civilian casualties? It's a natural question, given the Europeans' evident contempt for one of the purposes of the Geneva Convention [a series of international agreements establishing rules for the treatment of prisoners of war and battle casualties]: to deter un-uniformed soldiers from hiding among the civilian population—a practice that obviously makes it impossible for an attacking army to distinguish between legitimate targets and noncombatants.

Protecting Civilian Populations

In other words, the Geneva Convention seeks to protect innocent civilians by keeping soldiers in uniform, and by defining those combatants who don't wear uniforms as being outside the rules of warfare and undeserving of the privileges afforded to legitimate prisoners of war.

During the bombing in Afghanistan [after the September 11, 2001, terrorist attacks on America] we heard a lot from the Europeans about collateral damages, so it is strange that they should now turn around and be willing to overlook the chief cause of civilian casualties in Afghanistan: al Qaeda [the terrorist organization behind the September 2001 terrorist attacks] and Taliban troops [The Taliban was the Afghanistan government when the attacks occurred] who not only didn't wear uniforms, but actively hid among civilians.

One might even think that the Europeans would be especially eager to define al Qaeda and the Taliban as outside the rules of civilized combat, given (again) the Europeans' understandable concern with protecting civilian populations from the depredations of war.

But that, of course, would require following a consistent moral principle rather than simply a knee-jerk anti-Americanism: i.e., the Americans are wrong when they bomb terrorists who are hiding among civilians, and wrong when they try to follow rules to discourage terrorists from hiding among civilians.

This is just one of the aspects of the controversy over Guantanamo that is maddening in its absurdity and dishonesty. And—to pick out another thread of the European reasoning here—if our allies care so much about the Geneva Convention, shouldn't they insist that governments have to actually sign it to be considered a party to it?

The United States Respects Human Rights

Human-rights violations did not end with World War II. We still see genocide, repression of political and ideological dissent, disregard for religious freedom, class discrimination, persecution of ethnic minorities, unjustifiable emigration controls and inhumane punishments. All of these human-rights violations will be tragically expanded around the world if terrorists are not defeated.

So the United States has gone to war for the sake of human rights and freedom. This surely is a just cause. And America is respecting human rights even as she prosecutes a war to defend human rights—our military operations distinguish between combatants and noncombatants and use proportional force. On these criteria, the United States has performed admirably. Our precision weapons have spared innocent civilians and minimized collateral damage as much as possible. Clearly this war is a just war, as defined by St. Augustine and then by St. Thomas Aquinas.

Robert L. Maginnis, *Insight on the News*, July 15, 2002.

Not only has al Qaeda not signed the Geneva Convention, al Qaeda and the Taliban aren't even governments. Remember, it wasn't just the United States that said that the Taliban wasn't the legitimate government of Afghanistan, even the United Nations took that position.

At its heart, the Geneva Convention, as Cornell's Jeremy Rabkin explains, is about reciprocity between governments— you treat our prisoners decently, we'll treat yours decently.

Saying it applies to al Qaeda and Taliban prisoners is like saying the START II agreement [a weapons treaty between the United States and Russia] should apply to relations between the U.S. and Belgium, or—even more aptly—to U.S. relations with the Hell's Angels. Because al Qaeda and the Taliban are, in essence, armed, criminal gangs, and nothing more.

Also, if they really are lawful combatants, as the administration's critics seem to suggest, that would lead toward a nasty conclusion: that the attacks on the Khobar Towers, the U.S.S. *Cole*, and (maybe) even the Pentagon were justified acts of war carried out on legitimate military targets, and so the perpetrators can't be tried for their actions any more than a U.S. pilot could be tried for blowing up a Taliban arms depot. For crystal-clear thinking on these issues, the best source is Ruth Wedgwood, a law professor at Yale and Johns Hopkins. She considers the whole Geneva Convention controversy a bit of a sideshow.

Applying Customary Law

According to Wedgwood, even if the Convention applied (which she insists it doesn't), it still allows for interrogation of prisoners, doesn't require you to jeopardize camp security if it would be endangered by providing certain amenities (i.e., the Geneva Convention isn't a suicide pact), and allows for military trials.

Even many conservatives have been puzzling over the question of what body of law these prisoners would be tried under. Wedgwood explains that this area tends to be governed by customary law, especially the customs that have grown up around the Hague Convention of 1907 [which established rules governing the treatment of prisoners of war].

The Guantanamo prisoners can be held to account for "unlawful belligerency" (just what it sounds like), for violating "the rules of proportionality" (even if you attack a military target, it has to be done with requisite care not to kill civilians), and other violations of "the rules and customs of war."

What if none of the prisoners in Guantanamo directly participated in terrorist attacks? It doesn't matter. The Anglo-American concept of conspiracy is quite broad, Wedgwood says, and al Qaeda could easily be considered a "single purpose entity"—like a "Racketeering Influenced and Corrupt Organizations Act (RICO) enterprise" in the U.S.—devoted to murder and mayhem.

Simply joining al Qaeda would be the crime. Of course, the Europeans still need to figure out if it's that, or joining the U.S. military, that's the worst offense.

"Working conditions vary widely from country to country and from factory to factory, running from bad to inhuman."

Sweatshops Violate Human Rights

Gary MacEoin

In the following viewpoint, Gary MacEoin maintains that employees in *maquilas*—Central American factories owned by transnational corporations—are subject to serious human rights abuses. He contends that these workers, primarily young women, are paid less than half the amount needed to feed a family of four. In addition, MacEoin asserts, these employees suffer numerous illnesses, experience indignities such as verbal abuse, sexual harassment, and beatings, and have been prevented by their employers from unionizing. MacEoin concludes that the conditions experienced by *maquila* workers are a new type of slavery. MacEoin is a writer whose articles have appeared in publications such as the *National Catholic Reporter* and *American Catholic*.

As you read, consider the following questions:

1. What is the minimum legal wage in Mexico, as stated by the author?
2. According to MacEoin, from what illnesses are sweatshop workers most likely to suffer?
3. In the author's opinion, what will replace the nation state in the "new international division of labor"?

Gary MacEoin, "Maquila Neoslavery, Under Conditions from Bad to Inhuman," *National Catholic Reporter*, vol. 35, August 31, 1999, p. 12. Copyright © 1999 by *National Catholic Reporter*. Reproduced by permission.

L os Chinos dicen que los Nika orinan demasiado ("The Chinese say that the Nicaraguans urinate too much"). I heard this phrase repeatedly during a visit to Nicaragua [in January 1999].

Later in the month I heard similar comments in Honduras, but mostly about the South Koreans.

I had gone to Central America to find out what was being done for the survivors of Hurricane Mitch, the appalling storm that had killed thousands and left vast numbers homeless, many relocated to places where job prospects were minimal. The various governments were putting together ambitious plans to get new loans abroad and to spend them in ways that benefited mostly the small oligarchical groups.

An Intolerable Industry

For the displaced, however, the one concrete project was the expansion of the maquila industry, which provides starvation wages under intolerable working conditions. As President Arnaldo Alemán has expressed it, the maquila industry provides "the opportunity to convert Nicaragua into one big free zone."

It was in this context that the comment about the Chinese—actually Taiwanese—maquila owners, was made. Many maquilas allow the workers, nearly all women, to go to the toilets (which they keep locked), only twice in an eight-hour day, each visit for one minute.

Living as I do not far north of our border with Mexico, I had some knowledge of the maquila (or maquiladora) industry. There are hundreds in clusters around Ciudad Juarez, Nogales and Tijuana. They number 3,000 in all Mexico, employing over a million workers. The minimum legal wage, which is what most workers earn, is 34 pesos, (about $3.53) for an eight-hour day, about $78 a month.

Working conditions vary widely from country to country and from factory to factory, running from bad to inhuman. As a general rule, the worker earns the minimum legal salary in each country. Many maquilas pay by task, in which case it may take 10 or more hours to meet the quota for eight hours. A typical quota for a woman is to iron 1,200 shirts, standing, in a 9-hour day.

The industry has become widespread in Central America over the past 20 years. El Salvador has the greatest number of maquilas (240) and of workers (41,800). It also has the highest wages, an average of $129 a month. Honduras follows with 156 maquilas, 70,000 workers and an average salary of $83. Guatemala has 134, 70,000 and $81 respectively.

Nicaragua is in last place, in part because the Sandinista government, 1979–90, did not allow them. It now has 19 maquilas, 10,800 workers, and $64 monthly salary. Women constitute more than 80 percent of the maquila work force. (Figures are for 1996 and are approximate; statistics vary widely. In addition, the "average" salary reflects a work week that often exceeds 60 hours).

An Unhealthy Environment

In Central American countries the minimum wage amounts to less than half the *canasta basica*, the income needed to feed a family of four. It does not include rent, utilities, clothing, health or recreation.

Ironically, while maquila employment had grown to 200,000 workers in Central America (1996), this had made only a slight impact on massive unemployment. Between 80 and 90 percent are new workers, women and children who were not previously in the labor force.

Applicants for employment are screened carefully. The younger, and therefore less likely to complain, the better. Even 14-year-olds are accepted if they say they are 16. Over 24, rejected. If "too fat," rejected. Proof that the woman is not pregnant is demanded. Pregnancy is in most maquilas a cause for firing. Some maquilas in Honduras, according to Charles Kernaghan, director of the New York–based National Labor Committee, periodically give shots of the contraceptive Depro Provera, saying it is for tetanus.

There is no written contract. Workers can be fired arbitrarily and without notice. Many maquilas fire a worker before she becomes entitled to vacation time or the extra month's salary due in December. There is thus a constant movement from one employer to another. A worker who attempts to form a union or is otherwise "a problem" goes on a blacklist that is shared with others.

Few survive the unhealthy working conditions, poor ventilation, lint-heavy air and the harassment, verbal abuse, strip searches and sexual harassment for more than six or seven years. Doctors say most common illnesses are allergies, abortions, depression and tuberculosis. They report pronounced bronchial hyperactivity and asthma from the cloth dust.

Anderson. © 1997 by Kirk Anderson. Reprinted with permission.

Newspapers in Honduras in June 1997 headlined a collective hysteria in a maquila in Choloma when a hundred women fainted. While the employers claimed that it was simply a trick by the workers to get more pay, doctors insisted it was caused by poor ventilation coupled with undernourishment. A more general indictment of maquila conditions in Honduras was made in a 1997 report of the Honduran Committee for Defense of Human Rights (CODEH). It said 40 percent of employees were physically punished by pushing, beatings, blows on the head, whipping and being made to wait under a burning sun.

The Struggle to Form Unions

Governments make almost no effort to inspect for violations. Fines are nominal. When two Korean supervisors in a maquila in Guatemala were sentenced to 30 days in jail for physical abuse of workers, the sentences were commuted to payment of 5 quetzals (83 cents) a day, plus civil penalties of 75 quetzals ($12.50).

Consistent with the philosophy of neoliberalism, maquilas everywhere actively fight all attempts to form trade unions. Spies report on any efforts even to get together to discuss problems. Suspected leaders are fired and blacklisted. Members of the National Labor Committee, a human rights advocacy group based in New York, posing as investors, visited a Best Form maquila in Honduras in 1992. Identifying themselves as U.S. entrepreneurs, they asked questions about labor relations. Unions create no problems here, they were assured, because a computerized blacklist "weeded out all labor organizers, religious or human rights troublemakers."

In the summer of 1998, the workers in Camisas Modernas, a Phillips–Van Heusen maquila, made history when the company signed a labor contract, the only one in Guatemala. It was the culmination of a six-year struggle backed by the United States/Guatemala Education Project and the Maquila Solidarity Network.

The victory was short-lived. When the workers arrived Dec. 11 to collect their Christmas bonuses, security guards blocked the entrances, and the 500 workers were notified that the factory was closed. Phillips–Van Heusen pleaded "surplus capacity" while admitting it would contract labor in other maquilas in Guatemala and elsewhere in Central America. The lesson for agitators and troublemakers was clear.

The Future of Sweatshops

Many groups are working to shame the transnational corporations who own the raw materials and sell the finished products under major brand names to insist on humane conditions for the workers. In the United Kingdom, the Ethical Trading Initiative, composed of nongovernmental organizations, companies and trade unions, has agreed to a code based on International Labor Organization standards.

Prodded by labor and religious groups, the White House [in 1998] convened a Task Force to End Sweatshops. Nike, Reebok, Liz Claiborne and other major apparel companies participated, as well as labor unions and the Interfaith Center for Corporate Responsibility. After long and bitter haggling, the Apparel Industry Partnership produced a code of conduct and monitoring that the White House found satisfactory but which the labor and religious organizations rejected. It allows companies to choose their own monitors, does not require them to disclose the factories they use, or what factories they are monitoring. In addition, it lacks the International Labor Organization standards incorporated into the British code.

Here, then, is the neoliberal future for the "surplus population" of the world of poverty. This new international division of labor means the replacement of the national state by transnational corporations that swear fealty to no one. It means superexploitation of the helpless, the atomization of society, atrophy of the family and proletarianization of all culture. It is neoslavery.

"*Political and social modernization . . . can follow the economic development that apparel companies gladly bring to the third world.*"

Sweatshops Do Not Violate Human Rights

Scott Rubush

Sweatshops benefit Third World nations, Scott Rubush asserts in the following viewpoint. According to Rubush, student activists are wrong to protest American companies, such as Nike and Reebok, which contract work to these factories. He argues that many corporations have improved the conditions at these shops, including increasing wages and ending the use of child labor. Rubush also claims that the presence of transnational corporations in developing nations helps modernize the political and social structure of those countries, which benefits the populace. Rubush is a grant writer and the publisher emeritus of the *Carolina Review*.

As you read, consider the following questions:

1. As stated by Rubush, what are some of the demands of student activists who protest sweatshops?
2. According to a *New York Times* article cited by the author, how does the salary for a Nike worker in Vietnam compare to the nation's average annual income?
3. How did Phil Knight respond to the University of Oregon's decision to join the Workers' Rights Consortium, as explained by Rubush?

Scott Rubush, "Sweating It," *Heterodoxy*, vol. 8, September/October 2000, pp. 1, 11. Copyright © 2000 by the Center for the Study of Popular Culture. Reproduced by permission.

S tudents at the University of North Carolina had a rude awakening when about 75 student protesters occupied an administrative building on the school's main quad and demanded stricter guidelines for the labor code governing the school's apparel contract with Nike. The night before, signs had gone up and slogans had been scribbled in chalk on the campus's red brick sidewalks: "No More Sweatshops" and "This is the beginning of the end of global capital." A female activist stood in front of the building with a bullhorn and outlined the protesters' goals while still-sleepy students marched across the misty poplar-lined quad to their 8:00 A.M. classes.

"This movement is the voice of democracy," she droned. "It is the voice of moral conscience. And it is the voice of workers' rights."

The Latest Left Wing Cause

It was also the voice of the cause *du jour* on campuses all around the country. At a time when race and gender are yesterday's news, the alleged use of foreign sweatshop labor by apparel companies who manufacture athletic uniforms and collegiate merchandise is definitely in. It is an issue that allows an attack on campus administrators, a show of sympathy with American workers, and a solidarity with the anarchists opposing globalization.

Protesters' anger stems from the companies manufacturing collegiate apparel—Nike, Reebok, Adidas, and the like—who also dispense multi-million dollar licensing contracts to major universities. These companies provide cash and apparel to schools, and in return, the schools agree to allow a "Swoosh" or other corporate logo to appear on athletic uniforms. Apparel companies also gain the right to manufacture replica jerseys bearing the school name and logo. It may sound like a good deal, but left wing students have found a fly in the ointment.

That's because in recent years, these companies have begun circumventing America's increasingly strict labor codes and labor bosses by manufacturing these shoes, shirts, and uniforms abroad. In third-world nations like Honduras and Indonesia, factory labor commands a lower wage than in the US, so by contracting this cumbersome work to firms offshore, apparel companies save on their manufacturing costs. Student protesters allege that this arrangement amounts to "exploitation" of workers in the third world. Accepting the generous licensing contracts "taints" a university because the truckloads of cash and clothes that the schools receive were "manufactured in sweatshop conditions."

That has the student activists all over the country loitering in university administration offices during "sit-ins" and making long lists of "demands" for clauses in these licensing contracts. These include a "living wage," regular "inspections" of the third world factories, and membership in a watchdog group called the Workers' Rights Consortium (WRC). WRC's radical agenda has been endorsed by a spectrum of leftists ranging from House Minority Whip David Bonior to Noam Chomsky and by front groups such as the Freedom Road Socialist Organization and the Nicaragua Network. To date, students have cajoled 57 schools into joining the WRC, including Brown University, Cornell University, Indiana University, and the University of North Carolina (UNC)-Chapel Hill.

The Benefits of Third World Labor

The problem with this protest—aside from the trumped up, morally obtuse air it exudes—is the growing consensus that the use of third world labor has provided lots of benefits to lots of people. American consumers, of course, benefit from the "sweatshops" when they lace up cheaper shoes. Universities obviously benefit as well when they allow apparel companies to subsidize their athletic programs—and indirectly, some of their classroom operations. And most importantly, although lost amid the din of the activists' bullhorns, is the fact that the workers in the alleged "sweatshops" also benefit.

As the *New York Times* reported in its May 16, 2000 edition, "a typical worker in a Nike factory in Vietnam makes . . . more than twice the country's average annual income." The article also notes the low turnover rates in these factories—a rate that remains below two percent each year. Independent auditors like big-five accounting firm PriceWaterhouseCoopers, moreover, have inspected many of the overseas factories and have cleared Nike and others of the "human rights abuses" with which American students have charged them. Furthermore, the apparel companies have taken steps to improve conditions at these factories. Nike says it has increased wages by 70 percent. Adidas disavows the use of child labor. And so on. These jobs may offend American students, but they remain popular among the people whom the activists claim to champion.

Some Benefits of Child Labor

In our time the argument between defenders of child labour and abolitionists is not presented as a conflict between the employers' right to use any labour at the cheapest rate they can get and the moral horror inspired by the factory system. The debate has been recast in ways that are more appropriate to the contemporary sensibility. So now at issue is the clash between those who see the Western model of a labour-free childhood as a necessary pre-requisite for a civilised society and those who defend the right of children—including many children themselves—to work. The former, and this includes many trade unionists, say that the employment of children depresses adult wages, which makes people poorer and drives more children to work. They see legislation as the best means of combating it, as occurred in nineteenth-century Britain. Abolitionists tend to see work and education as incompatible. Defenders of child work say that, despite conditions that are sometimes dangerous and damaging, children want to work. It offers them a chance for self-determination and responsibility. It gives them a function. The problem is the absence of suitable work, not work itself. In any case, children learn more in a work environment that provides them with skills than in a school environment in which they are taught a reach-me-down syllabus from an archaic Western academic tradition.

Jeremy Seabrook, *Children of Other Worlds*, 2001.

And the relatively high wage rates of these "sweatshop" jobs haven't been the only benefits of a corporate presence in developing nations. As Mexico's elections demonstrate, political and social modernization—the sort of modernization that "progressives" should applaud—can follow the economic development that apparel companies gladly bring to the third world. It's no accident that the declaration of independence on the part of the people of Mexico from the oligarchy of [Partido Revolucionario Institucional, or the Institutional Revolutionary Party] (PRI) party should happen just six years after the North American Free Trade Agreement (NAFTA) took effect. Before the document's ink could dry, American companies rushed to build factories in the dusty *barrios* south of the Rio Grande. The millions of dollars of direct investment by these companies—whose laborers, by the way, have been notoriously difficult to unionize—resulted in tangible improvement in the lives of thousands of people. And as their living conditions have improved, they demanded that their political system improve as well. With the election of Vicente Fox and a National Action Party government in July [2000], it did improve, despite the best efforts of leftists decrying the "evils" of *neoliberalismo*.

And Mexico's not alone. A comparison of export-driven countries like South Korea and Chile with their neighbors who have resisted globalization shows the benefits of globalization even more dramatically. But the anti-sweatshop set ignores these questions. They're still decrying the "rapture of NAFTA" as a rap group tried to rhyme while performing at a gathering of the Students for Economic Justice at UNC-Chapel Hill in 1999.

The Influence of Big Labor

Blindness to the realities of the "sweatshop" issue is not just a matter of the claustral moral smugness of the student left. It is also the case that while college students are doing the dance, it is big labor that is calling the tune.

Since 1996, the AFL-CIO has sponsored a program called Union Summer, which allows college students to intern with individual unions, including the Union of Needletrades, Industrial and Textile Employees. More than 2000 of these "Summeristas" have passed through this program, which teaches union-organizing techniques, according to an article in the *Chronicle of Higher Education*. One graduate of this program told the *Chronicle* how he and his fellow interns parlayed their summer experience into a nationwide movement of anti-sweatshop radicals: "We have a network of students on 150 to 200 campuses, and everywhere this is happening, they are running the same campaign.". . .

A Backlash Against the Protests

While many campuses like UNC remain deeply embroiled in the sweatshop protests, a backlash by apparel companies has finally begun. After about 50 students staged a sit-in at the office of the University President in March 1999, the University of Michigan stipulated a laundry list of student "demands" while renegotiating its $24 million contract with Nike. The company called Michigan's bluff and abruptly broke off the talks. "This is not about limiting academic freedom or exerting influence over what monitoring organizations a university chooses to join," said Nike's director of college sports marketing Kit Morris in a statement following the decision. "It's about possibly subjecting our company to standards that neither we, nor our competitors, or even the University of Michigan and its vendors can honestly adhere to."

In an even more dramatic move, Nike Chairman Phil Knight [in April 2000] protested The University of Oregon's membership in the Workers' Rights Consortium by ceasing his own personal contributions to the school. Mr. Knight, an Oregon alumnus, previously had promised $30 million for the renovation of the school's football stadium. Mr. Knight said he was "shocked" at the school's ingratitude and backed off of the promise. "With this move the University inserted itself into the new global economy where I make my living," he said in a statement. "And inserted itself on the wrong side, fumbling a teachable moment."

These moves have caused schools to see that they can't continue the hypocrisy of having it both ways. And as push comes to shove, administrators have begun to modify their position somewhat to mollify the companies without annoying their students. [In summer 2000] the University of Michigan joined the Fair Labor Association (FLA), WRC's more moderate, Department of Labor–created counterpart. Conceding Nike's main complaint, University of Michigan spokesman Joel Seguine said, "We think it's wise to include the points of view of both groups. Including all points of view is the only way to solve this situation."

Despite these moves, Mr. Seguine says the university's overall policy remains unchanged: "We agree fundamentally with the students' position. There's just some disagreement about how to get there." Moreover, the university refuses to question the degree to which protesters have been performing from organized labor's script. "I think [the link] is perfectly legitimate in a democratic society," said Mr. Seguine.

The University of Oregon also has backed off its position somewhat, by forming a committee to review the labor code that sparked Phil Knight's ire last spring. On September 19, 2000, the university announced that it had also balanced its membership in the radical WRC by joining the moderate FLA.

Perhaps more funders like Knight should come forward to "maximize the contradictions," as the student protesters' Marxist forbears would have said. In American higher education today the only thing that can possibly trump moral humbuggery is greed. And the only thing that might make administrators stand up against left wing students is a cut in their budget.

> *"The majority of countries in Beijing endorsed the priority of international human rights for women over national and customary law."*

Human Rights for Women Are Receiving Greater Attention

Temma Kaplan

In the following viewpoint, Temma Kaplan contends that grassroots women's organizations have helped bring greater attention to worldwide human rights abuses against women and girls. She argues that these activists have made the United Nations and women from industrialized nations more aware of problems in developing nations, such as sexual slavery and female genital mutilation. According to Kaplan, the efforts of these activists helped lead to the achievements of the Beijing Conference of 1995, where the majority of the participating nations supported the importance of international human rights for women. Kaplan is an activist, historian, and author of three books, including *Crazy for Democracy: Women's Grassroots Movements*.

As you read, consider the following questions:
1. When and where did the "Decade of Women" begin, in Kaplan's opinion?
2. According to the author, what has the role of southern African women been in the battle for human rights for women?
3. What is the "new language of human rights," according to Kaplan?

U ntil the 1990s, discussions of human rights focused on torture and genocide and other extreme forms of abuse. The term "human rights" usually referred to violations of people's bodily integrity by agents of the state. Indeed there have been far too many instances of such violations in Argentina, Chile, Guatemala, Northern Ireland, Bosnia, Rwanda, and South Africa, resulting in torture and murder. But women grassroots activists, including survivors of such atrocities, have increasingly extended the term "human rights" to indicate a location and a process of direct democracy by which people reveal secrets those in power wish to hide. They include under the rubric of "human rights" opposition to various forms of violence, including economic and social inequalities against which activists have increasingly been struggling.

In the 1990s grassroots women's organizations pressured the official human rights organizations to discount the apparent separation between public and private life and to characterize as human rights abuses such violent acts as female genital mutilation, enslaving servants and child prostitutes, dowry death, domestic abuse, and the use of rape as a strategy of war. They have led marches and invasions of buildings worldwide to force the United Nations, and through it member governments, to stop abetting the abuse of women. Women's international social movements, basing their strategies on participatory democracy, on leading by pedagogy, and on integrating everyday life and politics to meet human needs, periodically express themselves through mobilizations, by which they have redefined "human rights" to mean universal social transformation. . . .

A Turning Point in Beijing

The Decade of Women began in 1975 with a meeting in Mexico City that brought women's grassroots movements into public view. Following that were UN conferences on women in Copenhagen in 1980, in Nairobi in 1985, and in Beijing in 1995. In addition, women, first led in this effort by Bella Abzug's Women's Congress for a Healthy Planet at the 1991 UN Earth Summit in Rio de Janeiro, have liberated space at all UN meetings (and at the would-be-secret meeting of the World Trade Organization in Seattle). Grassroots women's groups, lobbying official delegations representing states, have been participating in UN conferences by organizing simultaneous tribunals and forums. At the UN Conference on Human Rights held in Vienna, grassroots women dramatically invaded the hall where delegates were meeting and presented a petition signed by 300,000 women, organized through the Center for Women and Global Leadership. With this demonstration, grassroots women forced the delegates to recognize that violence against women in all its forms—including the use of rape as a form of torture, holding women and girl children in sexual slavery, or killing women because their dowries were insufficient—is a violation of women's human rights. Facing down the delegates, grassroots women from around the world made visible with their own bodies the invisible violence against women taking place all over the world.

The Beijing Conference of 1995 brought the world's women together beyond nationalism to formulate an international agenda. At the First World Conference of Women, in Mexico City in 1975, feminists such as Betty Friedan and women's grassroots activists such as the Bolivian mining-community leader Domitila Barrios de Chungara publicly argued about what women needed and whether middle-class women from the industrialized countries had anything in common with those from poor nations. In Beijing the effort to define women's rights as human rights bridged the gap.

At the other Women's Conferences in Mexico, Copenhagen, and Nairobi, Arab women and Israeli women locked horns as did other antagonists. Nationalist issues had frequently predominated over international goals; but since Beijing, the worlds converged, and the motto of "Women's Rights as Human Rights" has defined the relationship between feminists and members of grassroots movements of women—a pact that increasingly appears in joint public demonstrations. By creating a third space that is neither public nor private, grassroots activists have opened up an arena in which human dignity, not national law or custom, prevails.

The Beijing Conference marked a turning point. Women from Zimbabwe, Zambia, and South Africa, who marched as

91

a group, brought the experiences of grassroots legal and medical movements together. Having discovered that 42 percent of women in Sub-Saharan Africa report that they are beaten regularly and that nearly 100 million African girl children are victims of genital mutilation, southern African women activists publicized these practices not as individual and cultural problems but as violations of human rights for which the United Nations and participating states should be held responsible. Women from southern Africa led the struggle to view mistreatment of women in universal terms that make such treatment unacceptable whatever the religious, cultural, and traditional justifications. Effectively, these women and the majority of other participants challenged the notions that cultural context determines women's needs for bodily integrity. Women grassroots leaders from all over the world attempted collectively to supplant cultural

Nations That Have Ratified the Convention on the Elimination of All Forms of Discrimination Against Women (CEDAW)

Country	Year of Ratification
Australia	1983
Austria	1982
Belarus	1981
Belgium	1985
Bosnia and Herzegovina	1993
Bulgaria	1982
Canada	1981
Croatia	1992
Czech Republic	1993
Denmark	1983
Estonia	1991
Finland	1986
France	1983
Germany	1985
Greece	1983
Hungary	1980
Iceland	1985
Ireland	1985
Italy	1985
Japan	1985

United Nations Statistics Division, *The World's Women 2000*, 2000.

differences with universal ethical human standards applicable to all women.

Women involved in environmental justice movements around the globe took up issues about sustainable development and about how so-called globalization really meant globalization of markets, not of human needs for water, a clean environment, or access to public resources. In fact, activists from many continents discussed how trees necessary to maintain the water table were being leased to corporations, which deforested the land. They discussed how it might be possible to target certain companies that pollute several continents; grassroots women activists contemplated suing those companies in some countries, boycotting them in others, striking against them in other places where the rights of labor were relatively protected. With so many activists gathered together, women discussed the ways even progressive companies such as an American conglomerate, which provided canvas shopping bags to all participants of the Beijing Women's Conference, in fact employed women in sweat shops. The participants from the forum issued a public statement, chastising the company and shaming it in public. The company later agreed to raise wages and provide toilets for its workers. Although the conversations and programs of activists may be ephemeral—finding their ultimate expression in movements far away and years later—the document produced by official government representatives, the Beijing Platform for Action, represents some of the goals and strategies developed among the activists at the forum.

Key Goals and Strategies

The Beijing Platform for Action, passed by 132 of the 185 governments participating in Beijing, placed increased emphasis on a broad spectrum of economic and social as well as political demands as part of human rights. The Platform for Action called for an end to gender discrimination in education by the year 2005; it demanded that women hold at least 30 percent of all decision-making positions in government; but it did not set targets for reducing the "feminization of poverty," or for controlling the World Trade Organization, the International Monetary Fund, or the World Bank. Despite the difficulties of holding governments accountable to their pledges, the ethical issues raised in Beijing go to the heart of what politics will be in the twenty-first century. Although feminist theorists such as Denise Riley and Iris Marion Young have considered the problem of whether we can speak of "women" at all—given that differences of class, race, ethnicity, ability and disability, and sexual preference confer identities that are steadily gaining currency—grassroots leaders attempt to blur differences in favor of universal human rights.

While feminist lawyers have written the language of rights for women in national as well as UN documents, grassroots women activists have been less constrained by the language of existing legal systems. Women in grassroots movements want individual rights, but they also demand greater protection for the communities for which they speak. In other words, they want to transform international priorities to fulfill human need despite what customary laws or legal systems may dictate, and despite the agreements that so-called neoliberal or late capitalist governments have made.

Perhaps most important, the majority of countries in Beijing endorsed the priority of international human rights for women over national and customary law. A new language of human rights has been developing at the United Nations conferences in Vienna, Cairo, and Beijing. This idea about human rights attempts to transcend national boundaries to talk about universal human rights, with the emphasis on "human" rather than on "rights." They propose to go beyond national law, culture, religions, practices, and customs. At the preparatory conference for Beijing +5, held in New York in late February and early March 2000, the representatives of the 132 signatories to the Beijing Document began discussing what standards they will use to evaluate the progress they have made toward fulfilling their commitments. Conference of Nongovernmental Organizations (CONGO), Women's Environment and Development Organization (WEDO), and the Center for Women and Global Leadership have helped brief groups from all over the world who came to New York to lobby official governments to represent the interests of ordinary women. Activists have established a model for combining direct and representative democracy that goes to the heart of what democracy might mean in the twenty-first century. By providing mechanisms to have women at the base advise government representatives, the Center for Women and Global Leadership establishes a new form of representation that can keep women's human rights at the forefront. Women increasingly advise the delegates directly through their mobilizations. In such institutions, democracy blends with activism in pursuit of human rights.

Members of grassroots women's movements also gathered to make their presence felt at every meeting. Certain women have argued for years that gender must be considered not only in areas where equity for women seems obvious but also in areas, such as government budgets, tax codes, penal codes, and trade agreements, that might at first seem gender neutral. At the preparatory conference for Beijing +5, women lobbied governments to make sure they recognized that gender transcended social relations and that gender must be incorporated in economic and political concerns.

Activism and Accountability

The effort grassroots women's groups have devoted to articulating women's human rights not only creates a new universal claim, it also demands that the government go beyond the boundaries between what used to be considered public and private life. If enacted as national law, the force of the state could come into play against the vagaries of religions and customary practices and the brutality of individual family members. Authorities become responsible for protecting women against violence, rather than permitting women and their defenders to demand protection. Some fear that state intervention might infantilize women just when they need to empower themselves. And, as feminist activists have always worried, such growth in state power, which blurs the separation of civil society from the state, could put governments squarely back into the bedroom. Will this ultimately help or hurt women and gays? What must we do to gain the benefits of state support while keeping the state at bay?

It might be argued that, in any case, international politicians only pay lip service to ethical goals while they carry out business as usual. Yet consider the Convention on the Elimination of All Forms of Discrimination Against Women (CEDAW), written in 1979, passed by the UN in 1985, and endorsed by 135 countries, but not by the United States. The CEDAW amounts to an international equal rights amendment and has had an enormous impact on the countries that have passed it. They must now survey their own accomplishments and failures and explain how they plan to improve their records.

Instead of depending on hereditary or elected officials chosen to represent states at United Nations conferences, women working for reproductive rights, against sexual slavery, and for accountability about women's access to scarce resources such as land and water can advise the diplomats directly. No longer satisfied with working through the somewhat blocked arteries of representative government, women's international grassroots movements have been arguing with their bodies to add an element of direct democracy to the international struggle for human rights. In embryonic institutions, direct democracy blends with activism in pursuit of human rights. When such women lobby diplomats directly through their mobilizations, they effectively create a fourth estate: one that is neither judicial, legislative, nor executive. In such practices, democracy blends with activism in pursuit of human rights.

"Laws and practices governing women's personal status—their legal capacity and role in the family—continued to deny women rights."

Human Rights for Women Have Not Improved

Human Rights Watch

Women still suffer numerous human rights violations, Human Rights Watch (HRW) maintains in the following viewpoint. According to the organization, women throughout the world, especially in South America, Africa, and the Middle East, are sexually violated, denied property rights, discriminated against in the workplace, and given few rights in marriage. HRW argues that while the United States and Western Europe have taken steps to improve human rights for women, those efforts have been inconsistent. Human Rights Watch is the largest U.S.-based human rights organization.

As you read, consider the following questions:

1. According to Human Rights Watch, how have women been discriminated against in Saudi Arabia?
2. Why are women vulnerable to trafficking into forced labor, according to the authors?
3. What are some of the inequities in Syrian marriages, as stated by Humans Rights Watch?

Human Rights Watch, "Human Rights Watch World Report 2002: Women's Human Rights," www.hrw.org, 2002. Copyright © 2002 by Human Rights Watch. Reproduced by permission.

One of the greatest challenges of governments in 2001 was to make respect for women's rights a more permanent and central part of the international human rights agenda. Women's rights activists made notable progress on several fronts—leading governments to condemn sexual violence against women in armed conflict, holding governments accountable for failing to protect women from domestic violence, and forcing governments to acknowledge and treat trafficking as a human rights crisis. However, governments' reluctance to promote respect for women's rights systematically and thoroughly undercut these gains every day. Many governments' commitment to women's human rights remained at best tenuous and at worst nonexistent. The international women's rights community moved forward, pressing to protect women's bodily integrity and right to sexual autonomy, to examine the ways that race or ethnicity and gender intersect to deny women human rights, and to protect women from gender-specific violations of the laws of war.

The Taliban and Saudi Arabia

The September 11, 2001, attacks on the U.S. triggered an international debate about the motivation of the attackers and a just response. The subsequent U.S.-led military action against the Taliban in Afghanistan focused international attention on the plight of Afghans generally, and in particular on Afghan women. Governments in the U.S.-led coalition and those outside it argued that the Taliban's behavior toward women— including banning women from most types of work, forcing women to wear a head-to-toe enveloping garment, and banning women from education beyond primary school—was unparalleled in severity and constituted a systematic attack on women's human rights and dignity. Yet, while the international community recoiled at these abuses, the women's human rights record of other governments with similar practices, such as Saudi Arabia, received minimal criticism.

Critics of the Taliban virtually ignored Saudi Arabia, where women faced systematic discrimination in all aspects of their lives: they were denied equality of opportunity in access to work, forced to comply with a restrictive dress code, and segregated in public life. Religious police punished infractions of the dress code with public beatings. Kuwait's record on women's rights was also dismal: the Kuwaiti government denied women the right to vote, segregated them, and required them to veil in public.

The international community's lack of complaint about the women's human rights records in these countries underscored a reality that women's rights activists grappled with everywhere: women's rights must still be negotiated, and violations of women's rights often generate only fleeting interest. Many governments, through overt discrimination, attacked women's rights in ways that essentially stripped women of their legal personhood. For example, the governments of Nigeria, Kenya, Zambia, and other African states denied women equal inheritance and property rights. The Thai government denied women who married non-nationals the right to buy and own property in their own names. Egypt discriminated against women who married non-nationals by refusing to allow them to transfer their nationality to their children. Syria conditioned a woman's choice in marriage on the consent of a male family member. Although having no such restriction for men, Venezuela prevented women from marrying until ten months after a divorce or annulment.

Governments Fail to Protect Women

Governments that condemned some types of violence and discrimination against women often failed to prosecute others. Thus, Jordan and Pakistan condemned domestic violence but still offered reduced sentences to males who committed "honor" crimes against female family members. South Africa condemned sexual violence broadly, but failed to take adequate steps to protect girls in school from widespread sexual violence at the hands of teachers and students. Guatemala passed sophisticated domestic violence legislation but was content to let stand discriminatory labor law provisions that denied tens of thousands of female domestic workers equality under the labor code. Nigeria deplored the treatment of trafficked Nigerians abroad, but did little at home to stop domestic trafficking of Nigerians.

The international women's human rights movement functioned as the antidote to government complacency and lack of commitment. In every arena, women's rights activists challenged governments' cursory commitment to women's human rights. Toward the end of 2000, in part as a result of an ongoing campaign by women's rights and peace activists to highlight the particular insecurity of women in times of armed conflict, both the U.N. Security Council and the European Parliament adopted resolutions on women and peace-building, that explicitly called on governments to ensure that women participate both in peace negotiations and post-conflict reconstruction planning. Women's rights activists in Peru caused the government to modify its domestic violence law in January 2001 so that conciliation sessions between abusers and victims were no longer mandatory. At the United Nations World Conference Against Racism, Racial Discrimination, Xenophobia and Related Intolerance (WCAR), women's rights activists successfully worked to have the final document reflect how sex and race intersected to render women vulnerable to sexual violence in armed conflict and to trafficking, and reinforced women's right to transfer their nationality, on an equal basis with men, to their children. In mid-October 2001, activists rallied to press the Ethiopian government to lift a ban on the only women's rights organization advocating for women's rights in Ethiopia.

As governments responded to the September 11 attacks in the U.S., there was danger that a pattern of political expediency in governments' concern for women's rights would continue.

The following section describes key developments in women's human rights spanning a dozen countries in 2001. Our monitoring showed that violence and discrimination remained pervasive components of many women's lives. Governments both actively violated women's human rights and failed to prevent abuses by private actors.

Widespread Violations

As states and nongovernmental organizations (NGOs) throughout the world prepared for the WCAR, women's human rights activists explored the intersection between race, ethnicity, or religion and gender and the impact of this intersection on women's ability to enjoy human rights and fun-

The Enforcement of Chastity

Before reliable birth control, the practical value of female chastity and fidelity was based on the conviction that a man should support his children and their paternity should be obvious. After reliable birth control became available, female chastity lost its mandate in some developed societies, but became more rigidly enforced in some theocracies.

In extremist Islamic societies, pursuit of female chastity imposes the mandatory veil, enforced seclusion, and severe penalties for the flimsiest charge of female fornication or adultery. Penalties include prison, public beatings, and death by stoning. Culturally sanctioned "honor killings" of unchaste wives or daughters are common.

In pursuit of female chastity, the genitals of young girls are mutilated, particularly in Africa. The clitoris and/or outer genitalia are removed to diminish sexual pleasure and the resulting temptation. Even in the United States, the U.S. Health and Human Services Department estimates that 160,000 immigrant girls and women have been subjected to or are at risk of some form of female circumcision.

Lena Gomes, *Truth Seeker*, vol. 127, no. 1, 2000.

damental freedoms. As some of the cases below illustrate, women often experienced violations of their rights based on their race or nationality as well as on their sex, gender, or sexual orientation. Women experienced racism and sexism not as separate events but as violations that were mutually reinforcing. For example, soldiers and noncombatants subjected women to sexual violence in armed conflict not just because they were women but also because they were women of a particular race, nationality, ethnicity, or religion. Indeed, armed factions often portrayed acts of sexual violence against women in conflict zones as attacks on the entire community, a community typically identified by a shared race, religion or ethnicity. Likewise, women were vulnerable to trafficking into forced labor, not just because they were poor and uneducated, but also because in many countries their poverty and illiteracy was a function of discrimination against women of a particular race, ethnicity, or religion. But the impact of this convergence of racism and sexism did not end with women experiencing trafficking-related human rights violations; it also affected how government officials, such as police and prosecutors, in both sending and receiving countries perceived them. Governments treated trafficked women as illegal immigrants at best, criminals at worst. As a result, governments denied many trafficked women any meaningful access to justice or financial redress.

Women experienced widespread violations of labor rights because of their race and gender. In some cases, states created such varied categories of workers that some women were unable to prove discrimination compared to women of different races. They were also unable to prove discrimination compared to men of the same race. For example, in the U.S. manufacturing sector, white women may be employed in the front offices as secretaries and receptionists while black men may be employed in the factory, making it impossible for black women to prove discrimination because the employer hires women and hires blacks. But states did not just violate women's rights in the public sphere; they also persisted in enforcing laws and condoning practices that discriminated against women in the private sphere. Governments defended these discriminatory laws and practices as essential to maintaining the integrity of religion and culture. Numerous governments, as in Morocco and Peru, continued to uphold laws that gave women inferior legal status within the family and that violated women's rights to change or retain their nationality. Some countries, such as Syria and Malaysia, violated women's right to enter into marriage with their free and full consent as well as their right to dissolve a marriage on an equal basis with men. The motivation behind these discriminatory laws appeared to be to keep women from marrying men of a different nationality, ethnicity, or religion.

Women's Status in the Family

Laws and practices governing women's personal status—their legal capacity and role in the family—continued to deny women rights. While the type of discrimination varied from region to region, women throughout the world found that their relationship to a male relative or husband determined their rights.

Sub-Saharan African countries continued to use statutory

and customary law to discriminate against women with regard to property ownership and inheritance. The explosive increase in numbers of young widows with children as a result of the Human Immunodeficiency Virus/Acquired Immunodeficiency Syndrome (HIV/AIDS) pandemic and wars in the region starkly exposed the critical link between denial of women's rights and extreme poverty. Zambia provided an example of a country devastated by HIV/AIDS and extreme poverty where the majority of women continued to live under customary law that denied them the right to inherit property from deceased male relatives. Although Zambia ratified the Convention on the Elimination of All Forms of Discrimination against Women (CEDAW) in the mid-1980s, and its constitution outlawed sex discrimination, the constitution itself gave primacy to customary law in matters of inheritance. War widows in Sierra Leone faced similar prohibitions in customary law. In Nigeria, Ghana, Kenya, Uganda, and Zimbabwe, statutory law reforms over the past twenty years gave women equal rights to inheritance but judges in these countries continued to apply customary law.

Personal status laws in Syria and Morocco, among other countries, continued to curtail women's rights entering into marriage, during marriage, and at the dissolution of marriage. In Syria, the minimum age for marriage was eighteen for boys and seventeen for girls. If a woman over the age of seventeen married without the consent of a male guardian, the guardian could demand the annulment of the marriage if the husband was not of the same social standing as the wife, and as long as the wife was not pregnant. Further, a Muslim Syrian woman could not marry a non-Muslim, while a Muslim man had absolute freedom to choose a spouse. Syrian law also assigned different rights and responsibilities for women and men during marriage. A wife's "disobedience" could lead to forfeiture of her husband's responsibility to provide support. A man could legally have up to four wives simultaneously, while a woman could have only one husband. Women did not have the same rights as men to end marriage: while the personal status law provided for the unilateral and unconditional right of a husband to effect divorce by repudiation (the repetition, before the wife and a witness, of "I divorce you" three times), a woman seeking divorce was required to go to court and prove that her husband had neglected his marital duties.

The Efforts of Activists

Women's rights activists in Morocco continued their long-standing campaign to eliminate discriminatory provisions in the personal status code under which Moroccan women continued to be discriminated against with respect to legal standing, marriage, divorce, child custody, and inheritance. It appeared that, as was the case with the reform of the personal status code in 1993, the king would be the final arbiter on women's rights. On March 5, 2001, the King Mohammed VI formed a royal commission comprising religious scholars, judges, sociologists, and doctors to consider amending the code. In a speech on April 27, 2001, he reiterated his commitment to improving the status of Moroccan women and eliminating discrimination against them according to the Islamic sharia [laws] and the values of justice and equality. An advisory committee appointed by Prime Minister El-Yousoufi had failed to act on the issue during 2000.

Women's rights activists welcomed a long-overdue development in Brazil: in August 2001, the Brazilian Congress adopted a law that, after twenty-six years of protest and debate, removed the most discriminatory provisions of the 1916 civil code. Most significant, the new code gave both women and men equal authority in the family, abolishing paternal power, the legal concept that men had total control over decision-making in the family. Elsewhere in Latin America, however, laws governing women's roles in the family reflected entrenched beliefs within society that women are subordinate to men. The Chilean civil code continued to grant husbands control over household decisions and their wives' property. In countries such as Argentina, Mexico, and Colombia, the civil codes established lower marriage ages for girls (sixteen, fourteen, and twelve, respectively) than for boys, while women in Venezuela could not remarry until ten months after divorce or annulment, unless they proved they were not pregnant.

A serious consequence of limitations on women's equality

in their private lives, such as whom to marry, was loss of citizenship for themselves and/or their children. Nationality laws in such disparate countries as Egypt, Sri Lanka, and Bangladesh denied women the right to transfer citizenship to their children. These laws, designed in part to curtail immigration and thus maintain the purity, loyalty, and cohesion of the nation, demonstrated the way in which discrimination on the bases of national origin and gender intersected to further entrench women's subordinate status in the family and in society. Despite years of protest and lawsuits by women's human rights groups, in May 2001 the State Consultative Council of Egypt dismissed the parliamentary plea to amend the 1975 Nationality Law. Under this law, which contradicted the constitution, an Egyptian man could automatically transfer his nationality to his children while an Egyptian woman could do so only under limited circumstances: when the child was born in Egypt to a stateless father or to a father of unknown nationality, or when the child's relationship to his or her father could not be legally established. The Egyptian Center for Women's Rights estimated that thousands of women married to foreigners and as many as one million children continued to suffer discrimination under this law. . . .

The Role of the International Community

The war in Afghanistan mobilized international attention to women's human rights in that country, with the U.S. government and its allies giving women's rights a prominent place in the propaganda war against the Taliban. In 2001, however, there seemed to be a disconnect between the U.S. and the international community's rhetorical commitment to equality and a willingness to adopt and implement policies that fully integrated attention to women's human rights. In 2001, U.N.-sponsored meetings addressed critical issues such as the gender dimensions of racism, gender-based persecution as grounds for asylum, and an international protocol on the collection of forensic evidence in cases of sexual violence. At the same time, the U.S. and the European Union took steps on trafficking, international treaty ratification, funding for women's health, and trade that marginalized or ignored women's human rights. Women's rights activists found that many of these steps were tentative and inconsistent, and hoped that the international community's concern for women's rights in Afghanistan would be long-lasting and would result in stepped-up efforts to recognize women's human rights violations and curtail them also in other parts of the world.

Periodical Bibliography

The following articles have been selected to supplement the diverse views presented in this chapter.

Shanta M. Bryant	"The U.S. Needs to Sweep on Our Own Door Step," *Christian Social Action*, June 1998.
Arvind Ganesan	"Corporation Crackdowns," *Dollars and Sense*, May/June 1999.
Lena Gomes	"Women in Bondage," *Truth Seeker*, vol. 127, no. 1, 2000.
Duncan Green	"Child Workers of the Americas," *NACLA Report on the Americas*, January/February 1999.
Tom Hayden and Charles Kernaghan	"Pennies an Hour, and No Way Up," *New York Times*, July 6, 2002.
Henry Mark Holzer	"Hate: America Grandstanders in Rush to Defend Detainees," *Insight on the News*, February 18, 2002.
Charles Jacobs	"Stolen Lives," *Word & I*, August 1999.
Perry Link	"China: The Anaconda in the Chandelier," *New York Review of Books*, April 11, 2002.
Natasha Ma	"China's War on Women," *Toward Freedom*, March/April 1998.
Teresa Malcolm	"Amnesty Targets U.S. Abuses," *National Catholic Reporter*, October 16, 1998.
Ahmar Mustikhan and Massoud Ansari	"Women's Woes Under Islam," *World & I*, February 1998.
Vijay Prashad	"Calloused Consciences," *Dollars and Sense*, September 1999.
Eric Reeves	"Sudan: Humanitarian Crisis, Human Rights Abysm," *Human Rights Review*, April/June 2002.
Nina Shea	"A Worldwide Phenomenon," *World & I*, December 1998.
Nina Shea	"Europe vs. Human Rights," *Weekly Standard*, May 21, 2001.

CHAPTER 3

What Should Be Done to Stop Human Rights Abuses?

Chapter Preface

On December 11, 2001, China became the one hundred and forty-third member of the World Trade Organization (WTO). The members of the WTO, who generate more than 97 percent of international trade, are obligated to operate a nondiscriminatory trading system that requires that participating nations trade with one another. China's admittance forced the United States, a long-standing member of the WTO, to grant it permanent normal trade relations (NTR) status. Prior to that, the United States reviewed and debated China's status annually because of the Asian behemoth's spotty record on human rights, including its persecution of religious groups and restrictive population control policies. The United States had long reserved the right to punish China for human rights abuses by refusing to trade with it, but China's admittance to the WTO forced America to change its stance. In response, numerous human rights organizations protested the U.S. government's support of normal trade relations with China. However, many analysts have argued that as China becomes a larger part of the global economy, its human rights abuses will decrease.

Prior to China's WTO admittance, numerous free trade advocates had maintained that imposing sanctions on China would in fact worsen that nation's human rights record. In his 1998 paper *Free Trade and Human Rights: The Moral Case for Engagement*, Robert A. Sirico, cofounder and president of the Acton Institute for the Study of Religion and Liberty, writes, "Trade sanctions isolate the victims while strengthening their persecutors. Sanctions imposed in the name of human rights also serve the interest of domestic protectionists by limiting competition. The best policy for promoting freedom and human rights remains economic and moral engagement." Sirico asserts that human rights activists frequently ignore the important changes that have occurred in China as the nation moves toward a market-oriented economy. As he explains, "An economic miracle is taking place—a historic chance that the Chinese people will be made permanently free to pursue their individual dreams."

Richard Lowry, editor of the *National Review*, agrees that

trade can have noneconomic benefits. He cites Taiwan and South Korea as examples of nations that have developed into democracies as their economies have grown. Lowry suggests that China could follow suit: "In general, trade will create, from both foreign and Chinese businessmen, pressure to establish transparent rules for economic transactions—to create beachheads, in short, for the rule of law. Economic liberty, the rule of law, and privately held wealth are all crucial ingredients to political liberalization." Lowry acknowledges that economic growth will not immediately result in a regime change and may lead to some increased oppression, but he maintains that trade will gradually transform Chinese society and set the stage for liberalization.

Free trade is one of many economic, social, and political solutions that have been suggested to improve human rights worldwide. In the following chapter, the contributors evaluate different methods of ending human rights abuses. As the WTO illustrates, sometimes solutions to human rights abuses arise indirectly from international attempts to resolve other issues.

"If white people held today's black slaves, the entire human rights complex would be mobilized."

Slavery in Africa Must Be Eradicated

Charles Jacobs

Human rights organizations should do more to eliminate slavery in Africa, Charles Jacobs contends in the following viewpoint. According to Jacobs, slavery has been a serious problem in Sudan since the late 1980s. He asserts that Christian Solidarity International's (CSI) efforts to liberate Sudanese slaves have been wrongfully criticized by the United Nations Children's Fund (UNICEF). Jacobs also maintains that leading human rights groups, namely Amnesty International and Human Rights Watch, have acknowledged the crisis but have yet to follow CSI's lead. Jacobs is the president of the American Anti-Slavery Group.

As you read, consider the following questions:

1. How many Africans are enslaved, according to the author?
2. In Jacobs's view, why do the actions of Christian Solidarity International not fuel the Sudanese arms trade?
3. Why does the author believe black slavery has been ignored?

In the summer of 1998, Abuk Deng Akuei, a young girl from south Sudan, was enslaved after armed men stormed her village. Captured as booty, she was made to live as a concubine until January 10, 1999, when an American named John Eibner set her free. Slavery, today? Yes.

The Resurgence of Slavery

In a 1989 coup, the National Islamic Front (NIF), an Islamic fundamentalist party backed by both Iran and Iraq, took over the government of Sudan. Once in power, the NIF declared a jihad, or "holy war," on those who opposed the imposition of Muslim law or Sudanese Arabization; those who resisted could be murdered or enslaved.

The regime, which rules by terror, gives its militias uniforms and arms but no paychecks. Their compensation is war booty—crops, cows, women, children. Today, tens of thousands of Africans, most of whom are either Christian or practitioners of traditional faiths, are in bondage. Likewise, moderate Arab Muslims who resist the call to religious war have been terrorized, as have the African Muslim people of the Nuba mountains who resist Sudanese Arabization.

The first detailed account of a slave raid came from two brave Arab scholars from the University of Khartoum, Suleyman Ali Baldo and Ushari Ahmad Mahmud. (Mahmud has been imprisoned twice for his anti-slavery publications.) They investigated a 1987 attack on the town of El Deien that was part of the growing Islamic fundamentalist movement that preceded the 1989 coup. There, Arab militias stormed the village on horses and in trucks. They entered the church where terror-stricken congregants huddled, and attacked them with hatchets, clubs, knives, and guns, beating and shooting people to death. The panicked survivors were convinced by Arab elders that they would be escorted out of town to safety. Lured onto rail cars that were later set afire, people were either burned, shot, or captured as slaves.

Their fate is appalling. Slaves are either kept by the individual militia raiders or sold north. According to a State Department report, some are sold into Libya. While in Sudan, the slaves are given Arab names and taught to speak Arabic. They are forcibly converted to Islam. Girls chosen as concubines are genitally mutilated to fit into the culture of their masters.

The resurgence of a slave trade in Sudan over the past decade has been well-documented in the West. Investigators from Amnesty International and Human Rights Watch have traveled the terrain and extensively reported on the trade in black flesh. The U.S. State Department comments annually on the practice. Two United Nations special rapporteurs have issued several reports on slavery. Dozens of journalists have interviewed escaped or redeemed slaves.

The Efforts of Christian Solidarity International

Christian Solidarity International (CSI), a United Nations non-governmental organization based in Zurich, has been flying John Eibner and a few other fearless people into south Sudan for years. Bringing medicine and food, the flights are unauthorized and could be shot down. When CSI learned that families of the Dinka tribe were buying their children and women back from slavers whenever they could, Eibner helped negotiate a treaty between several Dinka communities and local Arab tribes. In exchange for being allowed to trade in Dinka markets, Arabs would send people up north to retrieve Dinka slaves. CSI announced at the start that they would never pay more than the customary price of the equivalent in Sudanese pounds of fifty dollars a slave, with the remaining fifty it collects going to cover the mission's cost as well as food and medicine.

On January 10, 1999, in an unimaginable scene filmed by CBS News and broadcast in February, Eibner handed over packets of Sudanese pounds to a slave trader for the release of 1,000 slaves. The liberated slaves, mostly women and children, were returned to their villages.

After this broadcast, a CSI spokesperson told reporters that the organization had continually asked the United Nations Children's Fund (UNICEF) to initiate a slave-tracing and retrieving program. UNICEF got annoyed. Three weeks after Eibner's action in Sudan, UNICEF offered its first comment about slavery there: "The purchase of a human being," UNICEF announced at a press briefing in Geneva, "is absolutely intolerable." This comment sparked an international debate between the world's preeminent protector of children and a growing, grassroots, abolitionist movement.

Responding to UNICEF

Spokeswoman Marie Heuze said UNICEF's condemnation was partly based on their opposition to sending "liquid cash, especially dollars" into Sudan, which only serves to "fuel the arms trade" there. This was wrong on its face. CSI redeems slaves with local Sudanese pounds. No arms trade is fueled. I called John Eibner to ask him about UNICEF's belief that what he does is "intolerable." "What would be intolerable," he said, "would be to leave the children in slavery. That they should remain where they are beaten, raped, mutilated—that is intolerable."

Nations That Have Not Eliminated Human Trafficking

Afghanistan	Kyrgyz Republic
Armenia	Lebanon
Bahrain	Qatar
Belarus	Russia
Bosnia & Herzegovina	Saudi Arabia
Burma	Sudan
Cambodia	Tajikistan
Greece	Turkey
Indonesia	United Arab Emirates
Iran	

U.S. State Department, *Trafficking in Persons Report*, June 2002.

In a subsequent press release, UNICEF Director Carol Bellamy elaborated on her agency's opposition: "The practice of paying for the retrieval of enslaved children and women does not address the underlying causes of slavery in Sudan, the ongoing civil war and its by-products of criminality. Until these root problems are addressed, there can be no lasting solution." Ms. Bellamy goes on to explain that "as a matter of principle, UNICEF does not engage in the buying and selling of human beings." But in its 1996 Annual Report, UNICEF proudly details how it helps mothers in villages in India redeem their enslaved daughters with cash.

When a WBAI radio reporter in New York put this to Peter Crowley, he stuttered that he was not aware of the program. What principle is violated when we help a Dinka mother buy back her child, but adhered to when an Indian mother is helped? Does paying for the freeing of Indian children address the root causes of slavery in the subcontinent? Surely not. I do not believe that UNICEF is a racist organization. And I do not believe that to Carol Bellamy the suffering of black children means less than the pain of lighter skinned boys and girls. Unfortunately, they have continually refused to discuss this with the American Anti-Slavery Group, as they refused to respond to this article.

It is true that some other groups copying CSI's work have caused trouble. Some have been convinced to pay more for the slaves than the standard fifty dollars. Some may even have been tricked into buying back people who were not slaves from Arabs who were not part of the formal program or cleared by Dinka elders. This has helped Khartoum attack the abolitionists, claiming CSI is causing the problem by incentivizing slavery! But there is no evidence that CSI's program has done anything but save thousands of lives and place the issue at the feet of the world. In fact, to protect the only program that has consistently and very carefully delivered thousands of their people out of slavery, local authorities in the four counties of northern Bahr El Ghazal—the slavers' main targets—decided to limit redemption activity to the CSI program alone.

Slavery Has Been Ignored

Perhaps UNICEF has taken its cue from the human rights community in general, which also has abandoned the slaves of Sudan. Where are the clarion calls for action from Amnesty International or Human Rights Watch? Why does it appear that black slavery is so far down on their list? The fact is that while these groups have done important and courageous work documenting slavery in Sudan, their constituencies are not easily mobilized to fight the oppression of blacks by non-whites.

The reasons go to the heart of Western human rights campaigning. Most members of human rights groups are white.

When decent whites see white people oppress others, they respond with moral fury. While there is a laudable moral drive to improve or correct the behavior of people who look like us, whites often become paralyzed when they glimpse evil done by people of color. Action against apartheid but silence on slavery exemplifies this dynamic. The impulse to scold the behavior of one's own group—white Westerners—is an excellent catalyst, though it is only the first step towards becoming a human rights activist. If the motivation stalls there, if we do not stand up for the human rights of everyone—no matter who their oppressors are—we have failed. The relative passivity of Western rights groups in the face of evil done by "others" has them abandoning victims whose tormentors are not white. Would Amnesty International want to be known as "The Society for the Improvement of White Conduct"?

Clearly, if white people held today's black slaves, the entire human rights complex would be mobilized. We would all do our duty and emancipate the slaves—by any means necessary.

Today, because of the efforts of American abolitionists from all walks of life, we are doing just that. The wave of emancipation that swept the West will roll forward, and there will soon be a time when all who are enslaved shall be free. And, as we know, the gift of freedom is priceless.

"Groups such as the American Anti-Slavery Group . . . are running against the tide of peace and progress in Sudan."

Anti-Slavery Groups Are Making False Claims About African Slavery

David Hoile

In the following viewpoint, David Hoile contends that the efforts of anti-slavery groups to eradicate the African slave trade are based on falsehoods and threaten the future of Sudan. According to Hoile, real slavery doesn't exist in Sudan; rather people pose as slaves and slave owners in order to get the reward that slave-redeemers are offering. He also asserts that the American Anti-Slavery Group (AASG), one of the leading organizations behind the redemption effort, has ties with Sudanese rebels and is biased against the Sudanese government. Hoile concludes that by spreading self-serving stories throughout the media, the AASG has had a negative effect on the peace process in Sudan. Hoile is the director of the European-Sudanese Public Affairs Council, which works toward peace in Sudan and seeks to improve understanding of Sudanese affairs within the international community.

As you read, consider the following questions:
1. According to an *Irish Times* article cited by Hoile, what people are often used to pose as fake slaveowners?
2. Why does the author believe that the American Anti-Slavery Group is partisan in regard to the conflict in Sudan?

David Hoile, "The 'American Anti-Slavery Group' and Sudan: Self-Serving Propagandists," www.mediamonitors.net, March 2001. Copyright © 2001 by Media Monitors Network. Reproduced by permission.

The new and significant moves towards a peaceful resolution of the Sudanese civil war, as outlined in the July 2002 Machakos peace protocol [which called for a referendum on self-determination in southern Sudan by 2008], must go hand in hand with a concerted attempt to cut away the dead hand of propaganda that has artificially prolonged the conflict. One organisation that has also been at the heart of the propaganda war surrounding Sudan has been the self-styled "American Anti-Slavery Group" (AASG). Headed by Charles Jacobs, AASG is based in Boston. Jacobs has confirmed that the American Anti-Slavery Group works closely with Christian Solidarity International (CSI). The organisation has been identified with claims of Arab "slave" raiders "enslaving" black women and children in Sudan, and has also been closely involved in subsequently discredited mass "slave redemptions". These sorts of "slave redemptions" had earlier been dismissed by reputable human rights activists such as Alex de Waal. As director of African Rights, de Waal pointedly referred to "(O)vereager or misinformed human rights advocates in Europe and the US" who "have played upon lazy assumptions to raise public outrage". He further criticised the use of "the term 'slave raids', implying that taking captives is the aim of government policy". De Waal stated: "there is no evidence for centrally-organized, government-directed slave raiding or slave trade".

The Fraud of Slave Redemption

In February 2002, as the result of some excellent investigative journalism, the *Irish Times*, London's the *Independent on Sunday*, the *Washington Post* and *International Herald Tribune*, chose to publish, or republish, articles exposing the deep fraud and corruption at the heart of claims of "slave redemption" in Sudan. These articles are the culmination of long-standing concerns about the activities of several organisations involved in what had become a Western-financed "redemption" industry in parts of Sudan. Claims by organisations such as AASG to have "redeemed" tens of thousands of Sudanese "slaves" have been sharply called into question. The *Washington Post* reported that in numerous documented instances "the slaves weren't slaves at all, but people gathered locally and instructed to pretend they were returning from bondage". The *Independent on Sunday* reported that it was able to "reveal that 'redemption' has often been a carefully orchestrated fraud". Rev Cal Bombay, whose Crossroads Christian Communications organisation in Canada had been involved in "slave redemptions", revealed that the Sudanese People's Liberation Army (SPLA) leaders such as Dr Samson Kwaje, in candid comments about "slave redemption", "doubted that even 5%" of the "slaves" had ever been abducted, and that "they were coached in how to act, and stories to tell".

The *Irish Times* reported, "According to aid workers, missionaries, and even the rebel movement that facilitates it, slave redemption in Sudan is often an elaborate scam". The *Irish Times* article also stated that in many cases "the process is nothing more than a careful deceit, stage-managed by corrupt officials".

"In reality, many of the 'slaves' are fakes. Rebel officials round up local villagers to pose for the cameras. They recruit fake slavers—a light skinned soldier, or a passing trader, to 'sell' them. The children are coached in stories of abduction and abuse for when the redeemer, or a journalist, asks questions. Interpreters may be instructed to twist their answers. The money, however, is very real. CSI can spend more than $300,000 during a week of redemptions at various bush locations. After their plane takes off, the profits are divvied up—a small cut to the 'slaves' and the 'trader' but the lion's share to local administrators and SPLA figures".

In an open letter in 2000 senior SPLA commander Aleu Ayieny Aleu stated that "slave redemption" had become a "racket of mafia dimensions". He also revealed, as an example, that one of his lighter-skinned relatives, SPLA captain Akec Tong Aleu, had been "forced several times to pretend as an Arab and simulate the sale of free children to CSI on camera". Aleu declared: "It was a hoax. This thing has been going on for no less than six years". This account, the *Washington Post* stated, "coincides with descriptions of the scam offered by Sudanese officials and Western aid workers, who said the sheer volume of money flowing into the south made corruption inevitable". The newspaper also reported that "prevalent fraud is acknowledged by senior rebel officials".

Charles Jacobs' Claims

In examining earlier, equally questionable claims made by the AASG, David Hecht, a British Broadcasting Corporation (BBC) correspondent based in Senegal, directly challenged the credibility of Charles Jacobs, bluntly referring to "the misinformation of Jacobs and his anti-slavery group". Hecht focused on claims made before congressional subcommittees in 1996 by Jacobs and the American Anti-Slavery Group which spoke of Arab slave raiders capturing black women and children in Mauritania. Jacobs testified that slaves are treated as "concubines". He also claimed that many slaves undergo exotic torture, including "camel treatment", the "insect treatment" and the "burning coals treatment". The congressmen were also presented with a receipt by Jacobs and his colleagues to be for the sale of a slave and her baby daughter.

The then Deputy Assistant Secretary of State for African Affairs, William Twaddle, stated with regard to the allegations made by Jacobs that they "have not credibly been brought to our attention". He stated, for example, that the American government had investigated the receipt for the "slave purchase" and concluded that the signatures were forged. Jacobs claimed that there were hundreds of thousands of black slaves in Mauritania. The State Department's country report on human rights in Mauritania for 1996, however, stated: "Slavery in the form of officially sanctioned forced or involuntary servitude is extremely rare, and a system of slavery in which government and society join to force individuals to serve masters no longer exists".

In his study of Jacobs' claims, Hecht interviewed Hindou Mint Ainina, editor-in-chief of *Le Calame*, one of Mauritania's leading independent newspapers, about the claims made by Jacobs. Hecht records that Ms Ainina scoffed at the stories of "slave raids" described to Congress and has never heard of the "bizarre" camel, insect or hot sand tortures cited by Jacobs. Hecht reported that "many in Mauritania believe these tales were concocted by members of

FLAM (Forces pour la liberation des Africains Mauritaniens), a liberation group for non-Maur Africans as anti-government propaganda". [FLAM translates as African Liberation Forces of Mauritania.] A senior U.S. Foreign Service official observed: "They [the rebels] have many legitimate grievances but slavery is not one of them". Hecht quoted Ainina as asking of American congressmen, "Do they think we have big plantations here and white mansions on top of the hill? They are sadly mistaken".

Redemption Encourages the Slave Trade

What seems to have kept the slave business afloat is the high prices paid by the slave redeemers. Though redemption prices also fell, they stayed far above the $15 paid in slave markets. Christian Solidarity International (CSI), according to its publications, paid the equivalent of about $100 for each freed slave from 1995 to 1997 and since then has paid about $50. In effect the redeemers are keeping prices high and creating a powerful incentive for raids. Some slave-redemption proponents argue that they must pay a risk premium—a sum sufficient to encourage dealers to bring slaves back to the south. CSI suggests that the premium is necessary to cover the costs of food, water, and armed guards to transport the slaves. "Traders incur substantial costs & serious risks for their own security," a CSI report from October of 1997 concludes. Fair enough—but no matter how the price for redeemed slaves is justified, the simple fact is that redemption makes the trade much more lucrative.

Richard Miniter, *Atlantic Monthly*, July 1999.

Jacobs has been accused of "Muslim baiting" and has referred to the Prophet Muhammed as a swindler. Prior to his involvement with AASG, Jacobs had been involved in ultra-conservative, pro-Israeli activism. He headed, for example, the 'Mosaic Group', described by the *Jewish Advocate* newspaper as "an activist group which countered anti-Israel propaganda in community organizations". When asked about Mosaic, one of Jacobs' colleagues stated: "Well, it's not the name that he [Jacobs] goes under anymore. I think that sort of fell by the wayside when he renamed it the American Anti-Slavery Group". In any instance, the AASG is clearly partisan with regard to the Sudanese conflict, supporting and working with the SPLA rebel movement. One of the AASG co-founders was David de Chand, a southern Sudanese rebel official. It has been noted that there is an ideological context for Jacobs' support for the SPLA. Israel had historically supported and given military aid to southern Sudanese rebels as part of policies designed to destabilise Islamic countries. In 2000, Jacobs became the Director of the Sudan Campaign, a coalition of anti-Sudanese groups. The similarities between AASG's claims about Mauritania and Sudan are clear. Just as in Mauritania, allegations about Arab slave raiders and claims of "slavery" in Sudan make for good anti-Muslim propaganda. Jacobs once again alleged the existence of "concubines". Allegations of "slavery" have been closely associated with, and have directly benefited, rebel movements in both countries.

Jacobs was also able to focus considerably more attention on Sudan by presenting the issue as one of northern Arab "slavers" and African Christian southerners. And in Sudan the whole issue has been a very lucrative one for "slave redeemers", with hundreds of thousands of dollars in cash allegedly changing hands. The AASG has also shamelessly exploited the naiveté of school teachers and schoolchildren as well as Harvard University undergraduates in its campaigns. In addition to claims of slavery, Jacobs has also described Sudan as a "terrorist, genocidal" state engaged in a "holy war".

Puff Pieces on Slavery

It has clearly been easy for the AASG to get its claims into print, particularly within local newspapers and television stations whose journalistic standards have been less than demanding. John Stauber, the founder of the Center for Media and Democracy, and director of "PR Watch", observed:

"Much of what you see on national and local TV news is actually video news releases prepared by public-relations firms and given free to TV stations and networks. News directors air these PR puff pieces disguised as news stories because it's a free way to fill air time and allows them to lay off reporters. Of course, it's not just television that's the problem. Academics who study public relations report that half or more of what appears in newspapers and magazines is lifted verbatim from press releases generated by public-relations firms".

This is precisely what has happened with regard to the "slave redemption" activities organised by the American Anti-Slavery Group. There is considerable evidence that Charles Jacobs and his American Anti-Slavery Group's carefully-designed "PR puff pieces" have found fertile ground in Boston. Jacobs has managed to secure national media coverage for his claims. The Boston ad agency of Hill, Holliday, Connors, Cosmopulos launched a campaign on behalf of AASG. Adverts were aimed at "grabbing readers with a provocative, even offensive, approach" and sought to place these ads in national papers such as the *New York Times* and the *Washington Post*. A senior vice-president at the ad agency, Todd Riddle, said of the ad campaign "[i]t puts a spin on the old slave auctions". The work of die-hards such as Charles Jacobs, and groups such as the American Anti-Slavery Group, direct beneficiaries of continuing conflict in Sudan, must be criticised for the self-serving activities that they so clearly are. They are running against the tide of peace and progress in Sudan.

"[Consumer] influence has been and can continue to provide improvements in social issues such as child labor and sweatshop exploitation."

Consumer Boycotts Can Discourage the Use of Sweatshops

Linda F. Golodner

In the following viewpoint, Linda F. Golodner asserts that consumer pressure can help decrease the use of sweatshop child labor. She contends that personal boycotts and other forms of consumer protests have helped improve human rights by convincing companies to establish codes of conduct that ban the use of child labor in the manufacture of their products. According to Golodner, consumer activism has also led several cities to adopt resolutions that ban the sale of sweatshop-made goods. Golodner is the president of the National Consumers League, an organization that works to increase consumer influence on market and labor issues.

As you read, consider the following questions:
1. Why does Golodner disagree with the assertion that personal boycotts cannot be successful?
2. What conditions have led to the flourishing of child labor, according to the author?
3. As stated by Golodner, what is the principle behind Bangor's Clean Clothes Campaign?

For over ninety years, the National Consumers League (NCL) has represented consumers who are concerned about the conditions under which products are manufactured. To illustrate the philosophy, an early League motto was the following: *To live means to buy, to buy means to have power, to have power means to have duties.*

Early Triumphs

In July 1940, Mary Dublin described the League's work as "an expression of the conviction that consumers have a far-reaching responsibility to use their buying power and their power as citizens to advance the general welfare of the community. Substandard wages and depressed industrial conditions impose a burden not on labor alone but on consumers as well. What is not paid in wages, the community is called upon to pay in relief; in wage subsidies; in contributions to meet the cost of illness, dependency, delinquency, and numerous other social ills which these conditions produce."

Since those early years, the consumers movement has blossomed into many areas of interest—from food/product standards and quality to consumer rights to consumer protection and more. New consumer organizations have expanded the scope and definition of consumer. But the consumer movement's history and mission (for some like the National Consumers League) reflect the continuing commitment and sense of responsibility for the conditions under which products are produced and for the decisions consumers make in the marketplace.

> Fifty years ago today a brilliant, though basically simple, idea was born. This was that the people who buy goods in stores could have a say as to the conditions under which those goods were produced. By their economic and political pressure they could fight child labor, they could protect women against exploitation, they could make the ideal of the minimum wage a living fact. (editorial excerpt on the NCL from the *New York Times*, December 9, 1949).

Consumer pressure significantly influenced the U.S. passage of child labor laws, minimum wage, and overtime compensation, as well as shorter work days and work weeks. Such efforts culminated in 1938's Fair Labor Standards Act. The League's nearly one hundred years of experience in fighting sweatshops and child labor underscores some basic truths which are applicable today:

1. Consumers should not expect a problem to be solved just because a law has been passed. When various industries, responding to the National Industrial Recovery Act of 1933, established codes prescribing maximum hours, minimum wages, collective bargaining, and abolition of child labor, the National Consumers League hoped its major work was accomplished. When the codes went into effect, the League kept in close touch with workers to find out how they were affected. It was soon apparent that in industries where unions were strong, workers benefitted through higher wages and shorter hours. But in unorganized industries, while there was improvement in hours and wages, unscrupulous employers used every possible device to rob workers of what was due them legally. (On May 27, 1935, the U.S. Supreme Court declared the Act unconstitutional.)

2. Consumers want an uncomplicated, easy means to identify products made under decent conditions. As consumer demand increased for such products during the early 1900s, the League developed and oversaw the use of the White Label. The label was attached to women's and children's stitched cotton underwear if the factory guaranteed that it obeyed all factory laws, made all goods on the premises, required no overtime work, and employed no children under age 16. Representatives of the League inspected factories to assure compliance. Originating in New York City, use of the label spread to 13 states. In 1918, the League discontinued the label as union leaders began developing labels that guaranteed labor standards enforcement. Consumers see labels as an easy point-of-purchase tool to use in the marketplace.

An Increase in Global Awareness

The concluding years of the 20th century have witnessed the expansion of the global marketplace and the propelling of companies to a transnational playing field. The consumers movement has responded with increased action and awareness outside of its own national borders to consider social responsibility on a global level.

Consumers who are educated about exploitative working

conditions and feel a sense of responsibility to act upon this knowledge find frustration in the marketplace. As a reaction to a lack of information and labels to help the conscientious consumer identify products made under decent conditions, many consumers are taking personal action—to include even personal boycotts of certain products, companies, and countries.

Students and Sweatshops

George M. Anderson: *Have students played a large role in the anti-sweatshop movement?*

Charles Kernaghan: Definitely. Besides the students who have helped [the National Labor Committee for Workers and Human Rights] with research on investigative trips, others on campuses have started active chapters of United Students Against Sweatshops. I give a lot of talks to promote this kind of response. In 1999 alone I spoke at 50 colleges and universities. For some of the talks, two workers from El Salvador accompanied me to describe to the students their firsthand experiences of factory conditions in their own countries. The workers and the students are about the same age, and the students could easily see the contrast between their lives and those of the workers. They'd say to themselves, "When I graduate after four years, my life will be in front of me with all kinds of opportunities, and I'm full of hopes—but what about these women in factories that assemble garments that bear my university's name, working for a pittance?" They quickly understand. We went to the University of California at Santa Barbara, for example, which is not known as an activist school. And yet 500 students showed up for our presentation. Now they're one of the colleges that have an anti-sweatshop chapter.

Charles Kernaghan, interviewed by George M. Anderson, *America*, May 27, 2000.

Some detractors claim that personal boycotts are doomed to failure through lack of massive consumer participation. The facts, however, suggest that consumers choose a personal boycott as a means of expression because they find a company's, industry's or nation's policies or behavior morally objectionable. In other words, their personal action is based on their commitment to not be an accomplice, even with a few dollars, in support of offensive policies. Thus it is not the consumer's worry whether their action will similarly motivate other consumers, but it justly can be the worry of the offending company, industry, or country.

According to the 1997 Human Rights Watch survey, "Because the goods purchased in one country may be produced by victims of repression in another, the very act of consumption can be seen as complicity in that repression." The expansion of the global economy is creating "new and immediate connections among distant people," and is thereby spawning "a surprising new source of support for the human-rights cause." To avoid personal complicity, many consumers "are insisting on guarantees that they are not buying the products of abusive labor conditions."

Over the years, consumer activism has influenced many industries. The results have been new product offerings, new labels, and new packaging. For example, the automobile industry was disinterested, often hostile, to providing airbags, anti-lock brakes, and other safety features until consumer demand necessitated their change of heart.

Consumer pressure for more healthy alternatives in fast food restaurants has culminated in consumers being able to go into any McDonald's today and get a salad. Consumers wanted more nutrition information on packaged food—especially detailed fat and saturated fat information—and they got it.

These examples reinforce the tremendous power that consumers have over industry. The same influence has been and can continue to provide improvements in social issues such as child labor and sweatshop exploitation. . . .

Industry Codes of Conduct

Media and consumer outrage over child labor and sweatshops spurred many companies to initial action within the last decade. In the early 1990s, industry leaders who developed corporate codes of conduct (primarily targeting their overseas contractors) were Levi Strauss, Reebok, and Liz Claiborne. Other companies followed, each emphasizing its own list of abusive practices that it would not tolerate.

On several levels, the company codes of conduct proved problematic. They fell short of their intentions, and thus lost their credibility among consumers.

Variation between company codes and standards bred confusion: Using child labor as an example as it is one of the issues most commonly addressed in codes of conduct, compare these differing definitions and perceptions of child labor:

• Levi Strauss says child labor is not acceptable and defines a "child" as a person under the age of 14 or who is under the compulsory schooling age.

• Wal-Mart will not accept the use of child labor in the manufacture of goods which it sells. Suppliers/subcontractors must not recruit persons under the age of 15 or below the compulsory schooling age. If national legislation includes higher criteria, these must be applied.

• JC Penney will not allow the importation into the U.S. of merchandise manufactured by illegal child labor.

• The Gap states that no person under the age of 14 may be allowed to work in a factory that produces Gap Inc. goods and that vendors must comply with local child labor laws.

• The FIFA (soccer ball governing body) code refers to child labor in the terms of International Labor Organization (ILO) Convention 138 (i.e., children under 15 years of age, as well as provisions for younger children in certain countries).

In word only, not in deed: Despite the introduction of codes of conduct, company implementation for the most part has been ill-conceived and ill-executed. Media reports, worker complaints, and persistent consumer concerns have underscored the ineffectiveness of the company monitored codes of conduct. It has become evident that words on paper and even the best intentioned internal monitoring is unreliable and inadequate.

Lack of transparency: Absent assurances from independent monitors and publicly available reports, consumers have little assurance that company codes of conduct are being meaningfully implemented and overseen.

Understanding Child Labor

Child labor exploitation is a global issue—with problems evident in over two-thirds of all nations. According to a 1997 report by the International Labor Organization, more than 250 million children between the ages of five and fourteen are forced to work in 100 countries, most performing dangerous tasks. Ninety-five percent of all child workers live in developing countries. In some regions, as many as 25 percent of children between the ages of 10 and 14 are estimated to be working. The Department of State's 1991 and 1992 Human Rights Reports and a 1992 ILO report attest to the growing numbers of children in servitude and their worsening conditions of work.

The problem is growing along with the expansion of the global marketplace. Child labor is cheap labor. Children are targeted for non-skilled, labor intensive work. Docile and easily controlled, employers have no fear of children demanding rights or organizing. Child employment instead of adult employment creates a climate where many children support their unemployed or underemployed parents and the entire family and their future families remain in poverty, ignorance, and exploitation.

Child labor flourishes under many conditions—cultural traditions; prejudice and discrimination based on gender, ethnic, religious or racial issues; unavailability of educational and other alternatives for working children; and no or weak enforcement of compulsory education and child labor laws. Globalization is strengthening child labor through providing ready access to areas of cheap labor that are rife with the above described conditions. Child labor increasingly offers an attractive incentive to keep labor costs down in a highly competitive global market.

Many U.S. companies have included child labor in their codes of conduct, due to persistent evidence of child exploitation in the industry. Although no definitive figures are available on the number of children working in the garment industry, the U.S. Department of Labor's Child Labor Study (1994) identified children working in the garment industry in most of the countries they reviewed. A direct connection was evident between these countries' exports and the United States, the world's largest importer of garments from 168 countries. "Child labor" does not refer to children working on the family farm or in the family business. It refers to employment that prevents school attendance, and which is often performed under conditions which are hazardous or harmful to children. . . .

Ending Sweatshop Abuses

An informed, empowered, and energized consumer movement is responsible for much of the progress against sweatshops and child labor abuses. In January 1996, the National Consumers League and the Union of Needletrades, Industrial and Textile Employees (UNITE) launched a Stop Sweatshop campaign, targeting both domestic and international sweatshops. The campaign's combined outreach represents over 50 million consumers. One goal of the Stop Sweatshops campaign is to equip consumers with the tools they need to send a "No Sweatshop" message to retailers and manufacturers.

"No Sweatshops" has gained new energy as public officials, city councils, and united consumers force the issue into the limelight in their hometown. Recognizing the advantages of citizen action and the greater responsiveness of local government, a new pressure point has been added to end sweatshop abuses. "If we can envision ourselves as a community of consumers rather than autonomous shoppers," says the Clean Clothes Campaign, "some remarkable things can happen."

Bangor's Clean Clothes Campaign: A city of nearly 31,000 residents, Bangor, Maine is working toward "sweatshop free" clothing within its city limits. Led by Peace through Interamerican Community Action, the Clean Clothes Campaign wants the city of Bangor to support a simple principle: Clothes sold in our community should not be supplied by manufacturers who violate established international standards regarding forced labor, child labor, poverty wages, and decent working conditions. They accomplished this in 1997 by banning the sale in Bangor of any item of clothing produced in violation of these most basic standards of ethical practice.

The campaign will next build upon the community consensus against sweatshops with a retailer campaign. Retailers will be pressed to take a pledge of corporate and social accountability to the Bangor community. The Clean Clothes Campaign insists that "ordinary people should have something to say about the behavior of businesses, large or small, that operate in our community. We would never permit local vendors to sell us rotten meat, or stolen property, or illicit drugs because such behavior offends our community values. Likewise, we do not condone international corporations supplying our retailers with items made under conditions that equally offend our sense of decency."

"FoulBall" spurs Los Angeles: The City Council of Los Angeles, California approved a resolution in December 1996, requiring the city to only purchase sporting goods that have been certified by a reputable independent organization as having been manufactured without the illegal use of child labor. The resolution has received tremendous support from youth soccer leagues, parents, and schools.

The effort was a response to the FoulBall Campaign to end the exploitation of children in the manufacture of sports equipment. It has become a model resolution for other cities.

Innovative Law in North Olmsted, Ohio: In February 1996, the North Olmsted City Council approved an ordinance forbidding the purchase, rent, or lease of goods which have been manufactured under sweatshop conditions. The law refers to the following when determining sweatshop conditions: child labor, forced labor, wages and benefits, hours of work, worker rights, and health and safety. A Cleveland suburb with a population of 35,000, North Olmsted's purchasing amounts to approximately $150,000 per year on items commonly produced in sweatshops.

Suppliers must sign a new cause on all contracts and purchase requisitions stating that their products are not made in sweatshops. If the city discovers a supplier does sell sweatshop products, the contract will be canceled or other appropriate action taken.

Twelve other cities in Ohio, including Cleveland and Dayton, have passed the same resolution. In Pennsylvania, Allentown has passed a law and Pittsburgh and Philadelphia are pending. Cities elsewhere who have the same law are San Francisco and Lansing. . . .

The heart and soul of the consumers movement is social responsibility. Sweatshops and child labor are not new concerns nor a new battle for consumers. Our expectations in company conduct are reasonable and attainable, despite the complexities of global sourcing. And, like our predecessors, we will not give up the fight until consumers—at a minimum—are given a clear and credible choice in the marketplace for products made under decent conditions. No excuses accepted.

"Advocates of consumer boycotts seek to implement in other countries a liberal vision that is increasingly discredited here at home."

Consumer Boycotts Are a Misguided Response to Sweatshops

Fred Smith

Boycotts and other economic sanctions against sweatshops hurt, rather than help, workers in developing nations, Fred Smith claims in the following viewpoint. According to Smith, boycotts limit the economic opportunities for families in Asia and Latin America by closing down factories or preventing children—whose families need the income— from working. He argues that urbanization and industrialization are needed to improve economic conditions in the Third World. Smith is the founder of the Competitive Enterprise Institute, which provides market-based solutions to public policy problems.

As you read, consider the following questions:

1. In Smith's opinion, what are the consequences of successful boycotts?
2. How has the American belief in egalitarianism been subverted, according to the author?
3. According to Smith, what is the goal of liberal protectionists?

Fred Smith, "Q: Do Consumer Boycotts Help the World's Poor? No: Well-Intentioned Boycotts Actually Make the Climb Out of Grinding Poverty More Difficult," *Insight on the News*, vol. 15, November 29, 1999, pp. 41–42. Copyright © 1999 by *Insight on the News*. Reproduced by permission.

S omeone once noted that the law was amazingly equi-
table—it forbids both the king and the pauper to sleep
beneath the bridge! And it is this form of equity that liberal
ideologues of the world seek to impose on those less fortu-
nate than we. Much of the world remains tragically impov-
erished—as the left when railing about income inequality
never ceases to emphasize. The one-fifth of mankind that in-
habits the United States, Europe, Japan and a handful of
other places around the world are vastly better off than the
rest of humanity. For most of them, choices such as whether
to labor in a dismal factory in a tropical backwater long have
disappeared into history but remain a tragic necessity for the
poor of the developing world.

But those choices are real and painful. For too many families in Asia and Latin America children must contribute
early on to the family income. These people lack the wealth
to delay the entry of their offspring into the world of work
until after they've gone to grammar school, much less college and graduate school. In traditional agricultural societies, children quickly move into the fields to work under the
supervision of a family member or friend in the village. Having grown up in a poor rural farm community in Louisiana,
I know well the results of that process—parasitic infestation
(hookworms or worse) resulting in poor health and inatten-
tiveness in school, early maturation and escape into early
marriage or the military.

The Importance of Increasing Wealth

We all can hope that the developing world will gain the
wealth that might allow their children to attend school, develop their intellectual capital and move into a more fulfilling adulthood. But increasing wealth is the vital prerequisite.
To ban a painful choice because we would prefer a better
choice is merely to push under the table the painful realities
these people face.

Recall Western history: It was only the Industrial Revolution that gave poor people and their children the opportunity to escape into a somewhat better world. The "satanic
mills" of England must be contrasted with the absolute hor-
rors of traditional rural life. People moved into the urban

sweatshops from the even sweatier life of farm serfdom.

Historical records show that average lifespans increased far more rapidly as urbanization and workforce participation increased. Families were able to afford some furniture, some tools, some reading materials, more than one change of clothes—pathetic accumulations but better than none at all.

Boycotts Do Not Work

The liberal scolds of the world love the symbolism of boycotting the evils of the global marketplace. America's chattering-class elites don't buy Reeboks or tropical-wood products or California grapes or an increasingly long list of products that are disapprovingly discussed at the cocktail parties of the rich and famous.

Yet the world isn't changed by symbolism but by reality. Such boycotts frequently are futile. And successful boycotts do nothing to increase family wealth in the developing world. On the contrary, the children who once were employed in the now-closed factories don't go back to school, much less aspire to college. Rather they go back into the fields or, even more tragically, in some cases become child prostitutes. Paternalism is far from unusual in the world—but does it help?

Boycotting the products of sweatshop labor is an attempt to dissolve options one wished didn't exist. It is the cheap out for the modern liberal. On the stateside economy this mindset leads to calls to increase the minimum wage—to ensure that everyone has a "living wage." But what about the person who now has no wage at all? As Doug Bandow of the Cato Institute pointed out, welfare recipients in states that have raised the minimum wage remained on welfare 44 percent longer than those in states that did not take this moral step. Conclusion: Raising the minimum-wage bar makes advocates for the downtrodden feel better but is actually bad for the poor. Minimum wages are bad policy at any time; in today's booming economy, they are especially costly. For the first time since WWII, employers are willing to reach into the ranks of the (once) unemployable, to make the investments in training that would give these people a real chance to gain economic independence. Minimum-wage increases threaten to reduce that hope.

135

Internationally, the same moralistic sentiments that lead to minimum-wage laws at home lead to protectionist policies abroad. American consumers are urged to boycott products from Myanmar because the regime there has too little regard for human rights. Our chattering classes talk smugly about trade sanctions, when in fact trade provides one of the very few windows available to the struggling citizens of Myanmar. Do the Burmese elites notice the effects of these sanctions? The Burmese poor certainly do. Or, we are told, "Boycott United Fruit and buy only Rainforest Crunch"— that will certainly fail to increase living standards in the jungles of Latin America.

The Damage Caused by Liberal Policies

Liberals are precious—their love is for humanity as an abstraction. Meanwhile, individual people must fend for themselves. Liberal policies may be motivated by moral values but, in practice, they do more damage than have any imperialist policies in history. Protectionist policies motivated by moral concerns curtail trade in exactly those countries most in need of openings to the world. Such moves deny the poor of the world the self-help measures that provide the first rungs on the ladder out of poverty. At best, the liberals would promote the dependency-producing welfare state as a substitute for trade. Liberals redistribute wealth; they do not create it—that requires sweat and liberals aren't into sweat.

And if the United Students Against Sweatshops get their way, the World Trade Organization, the only positive international organization, will become an arm of Greenpeace, Amnesty International and [consumer activist] Ralph Nader's brigades. Economic protectionists—labor unions and their corporate allies—have forged an unholy alliance with these groups. Protectionists have become cross-dressers—seeking to cloak their traditional special-interest cause in moral garb. They must not be allowed to succeed.

In effect, advocates of consumer boycotts seek to implement in other countries a liberal vision that is increasingly discredited here at home. It's as if they are saying, "The poor may not be able to afford our level of regulation but by God they're going to get the chance." And if progressivism fails there, too, and the poor are made even worse off, they can always say, "Well, we tried!"

Asay. © 1999 by Creators Syndicate, Inc. Reprinted with permission.

Progressivism no longer can do much damage here at home—Americans no longer are listening to liberal polemicists—but the poor of the world remain vulnerable. American supermarkets and department stores don't need to buy from Burma or tropical villagers or Bangladeshi school children. If a boycott is threatened, the Levi-Strauss firms of America simply will shift to a less controversial substitute. The producer won't suffer; the wealthier customers will never notice—although the working poor will find their choices narrowing dramatically. Most tragically, the thwarted dreams of the child in Asia will never be heard at all on nightly news. Instead, we will hear only tales of moral triumph from a compliant media. A proud Mattel will note that "we sell toys to children—we don't ask children to make toys!"

What Americans Should Do

Americans have a proud egalitarian tradition. As a child I was proud when a friend working in Latin America discussed his policy of paying local workers the same rate as Americans. His attitude—the traditional American view—is that merit, not ethnicity, should determine outcome. But that egalitarian view has been subverted into a form of radical egalitarianism which argues for equality of outcome—even when we have no meaningful way of bringing about that outcome. Americans should seek a world where children will not have to go into the fields or the factories, where they too will have the opportunity to build intellectual capital for the future. Tragically, that day is not yet. Today, people must painfully accumulate tiny amounts of capital through family efforts, and, for many, only open world trade offers them an opportunity to climb out of poverty.

America, of course, has its own special poverty problems. For example, some religious communities, such as the Amish, hold beliefs that make it difficult for them to participate fully in the American prosperity. Their traditional non-technological lifestyle makes it critical for their children to contribute to family income very early in life. And Congress has enacted laws to allow them to work at an early age under conditions that many of us well might find distasteful. Our reasons for doing so are understandable. Americans respect religious beliefs—even those we do not support—and we recognize that allowing Amish children to labor in their communities may help them reach responsible adulthood. Indeed, even strong opponents of child labor recognize that value. Representative George Miller, a California Democrat, noted that "child labor contributes to family income and can even train children for future work." In tomorrow's Internet economy sanctions against child labor take on an even more oppressive note because there is every reason to believe that even some school-age children will be able to leapfrog from poverty to prosperity by working at home on laptop computers. Do we really wish to let child-labor restrictions hamstring the Bill Gates of the next generation?

Sadly, leaders of consumer boycotts who drape themselves in the banner of a children's crusade will not protect the children of the world. It even may be argued that such is not really their purpose. Liberal protectionists' real goal is to protect their liberal sensitivities. How much more pleasant to ban all ugliness from the world. Boycotts, global child-labor laws, sanctions against developing-world products, minimum-wage laws—all are motivated not primarily by the desire to help the poor but rather to protect liberals from reality shock.

And to those who argue that we must increase the wealth of these people so that their children would not have to work, we must ask: But how? Show us a practical way of achieving that desirable result. To cut off painful options based on the theoretical argument that such choices should not be necessary is to assuage an elitist aesthetic concern at the expense of those who would have desperately preferred freedom to choose. Trade offers a slow escape from poverty. Feel-good remedies leave the poor anchored in place. But escapist fantasies are too high a price to pay for boycott policies whose only connection to civility and humaneness is their superficial attractiveness.

*"[Nongovernmental organizations] have
played an important historical role in
establishing and expanding the U.N.
human rights system."*

Nongovernmental Organizations Help Improve Human Rights

Peter van Tuijl

In the following viewpoint, Peter van Tuijl, a senior adviser
with the Netherlands Organisation for International Development Cooperation, asserts that nongovernmental organizations (NGOs) play an important role in the promotion of
human rights. According to van Tuijl, NGOs have helped
establish a variety of international human rights treaties and
conventions and have also supported efforts by the United
Nations to develop a global system of human rights. However, he argues that in order for nongovernmental organizations to become more effective, they must improve their
own accountability to the people they serve.

As you read, consider the following questions:
1. What are some of the issues with which nongovernmental
   organizations have been involved, according to van Tuijl?
2. As stated by the author, what are the three ways NGOs
   support the development of the UN system of human
   rights?
3. What universal values do NGOs promote, according to
   the author?

Peter van Tuijl, "NGOs and Human Rights: Sources of Justice and Democracy,"
Journal of International Affairs, vol. 52, Spring 1999, pp. 493–98. Copyright
© 1999 by The Trustees of Columbia University in the City of New York.
Reproduced by permission.

The United Nations–based system of universal human rights is one of the major achievements of this century. Codified in the Universal Declaration of Human Rights, it provides a normative framework as well as a source of inspiration for achieving justice and protecting the weak and vulnerable. In this viewpoint, I define justice as treating people and populations fairly and allowing individuals to participate in society according to their abilities.

The Growing Role of NGOs

Globalization increases the sources of injustice that are beyond the scope of national systems of justice. Today, forces that are geographically and institutionally distant from the scene of the action may influence individuals and communities. Multinational corporations and the Bretton Woods institutions—the World Bank and the International Monetary Fund—have a major impact on the lives of millions, but there are few local or decentralized institutional opportunities for recourse against their actions. The political space for governments is equally affected by international forces, which may have an impact on how governments behave domestically.

Nongovernmental organizations (NGOs) have begun to fill some of these widening institutional and geographical gaps for people or communities who want to exercise their guaranteed rights. Particularly during the last 25 years, NGOs have contributed to international and national discourse on issues of global scope, such as the eradication of poverty and the promotion of gender equality, peace, sustainable development and human rights. Most NGOs no longer work alone, but rather in networks that transfer information and other resources across borders. In this viewpoint, I explore the extent to which the gradually increasing density of NGO networks and intensifying degree of NGO advocacy can be seen as a nascent organizational articulation of a global human rights enforcement mechanism. Such a response would answer the traditional critique that the U.N. human rights principles lack sufficient organized enforcement mechanisms. The question is whether this anticipates a more institutionalized role for NGOs in emerging systems of global governance.

The study of NGOs and how their networks might be organized to enforce human rights leads to a qualitative discussion of the relationships among these organizations. This [viewpoint] explores the distinctive relationships among NGOs—as well as the relationship between NGOs and nation-states. It examines how effective they are in promoting human rights and to what level of accountability they are subject. I argue that if they wish to aspire to a more institutionalized position within the human rights system, NGOs need to further develop the quality of their networks to become innovative sources of democracy as well as legitimate and effective sources of universal human rights and international justice.

Defining NGOs

Nongovernmental organizations have grown remarkably in variety and number in the past 25 years. Though estimations differ, the NGOs listed in such resources as the Organization for Economic Cooperation and Development (OECD) Directory of NGOs, the United Nations Development Programme's (UNDP) Human Development Report and research based on the Yearbook of International Associations all indicate a significant expansion of the NGO sector. The UNDP report of 1993 cites 50,000 NGOs worldwide. Between 1980 and 1990, the OECD reported an increase from 1,600 to 2,500 organizations in its 24 member countries. It is safe to assume that tens of thousands of NGOs worldwide are currently covering a multitude of concerns and working either at or across the local, national or international levels. However, the distribution of these groups throughout the world is not equal.

When writing about NGOs and human rights in the global realm, one should recognize that conceptual or analytical shortcuts are sometimes needed. Conceptual difficulties emerge when one accounts for the academic and political debate surrounding terms like "NGOs" and "NGO advocacy," "civil society," "globalization" and "global governance."

In my discussion, I will use Anna Vakil's definition of NGOs as "self-governing, private, not-for-profit organizations that are geared toward improving the quality of life of disadvantaged people." They are neither part of government nor controlled by a public body. As such, they are elements of civil society, which is "a space or arena between households and the state which affords possibilities of concerted action and social self-organization."

NGOs and Development

The potential for human rights non-governmental organizations (NGOs) is significant in the field of development. While identification of development projects for specific populations requires the involvement of governments and aid donors, both of these entities face limitations and present obstacles when it comes to project identification—the crucial first step of any successful and sustainable development project. NGOs do not face the diplomatic restraints of governments when it comes to conducting needs assessments or publicizing problems; their projects generally involve participation from the intended beneficiaries; and they are much more efficient (partially due to their dedication and partially to their light administrative structures). Governments obviously operate according to politics, and while this poses enough problems in transparent democratic societies, it can spell disaster in authoritarian ones. . . . Both aid donors and governments may be too socially, economically, culturally, and geographically removed from the people who are being considered for development. When it comes to rural populations and even small cities that are distant from the capital, groups that consider themselves to be very distinct may be categorized together, resulting in counterproductive tensions and, most likely, a conflation of interests. It is in this representational capacity that NGOs can play a valuable role.

T. Jeffrey Scott, "Evaluating Development-Oriented NGOs," *NGOs and Human Rights*, 2001.

Globalization and global governance are equally broad notions. Globalization's impact is uneven and needs to be qualified in accordance with specific circumstances, such as the perceived erosion of the power of nation-states. Taking this as a given political reality, I endorse a definition of globalization or global governance as "efforts to bring more orderly and reliable responses to social and political issues that go beyond capacities of states to address individually."

I will discuss human rights in terms of the full scope of

economic, social and cultural rights, as well as civil and political rights. Distinguishing between the two sets of rights violates the reality of NGO work; on the operational level, NGOs are as involved in providing access to opportunities for physical and economic advancement as they are in providing opportunities for defining and exercising civil liberties. Although individual NGOs frequently have a particular mission that is more closely related to one of the two categories of rights, they have confirmed and strengthened the commitment to the indivisibility and interdependence of human rights as a matter of principle. "One set of rights cannot be used to bargain for another" was a chief element in the NGO contribution to the 1993 U.N. World Conference on Human Rights in Vienna.

Establishing a Human Rights System

NGOs have played an important historical role in establishing and expanding the U.N. human rights system. The role of NGO "consultants" in the U.S. delegation to the U.N. founding conference in San Francisco in 1945 helped achieve the inclusion of human rights in the U.N. Charter. Since the adoption of the Universal Declaration of Human Rights in 1948, NGOs have consistently continued their efforts to strengthen the U.N. human rights system and have succeeded in influencing the formulation of different U.N. treaties and conventions, such as the 1979 Convention on the Elimination of All Forms of Discrimination against Women and the 1989 Convention on the Rights of the Child. Often, NGOs have led the way in proposing new institutional arrangements in order to embody U.N. responses to human rights abuses. Their influence is visible in the creation of such mechanisms as the U.N. expert body to examine disappearances, the working group on arbitrary detention, the establishment of Special Rapporteurs—there are now Special Rapporteurs for nine different categories of universal human rights—to conduct expert investigations and, of course, the creation of the position of U.N. High Commissioner for Human Rights.

NGOs' support of the development of the U.N. system of human rights can be summarized by three functions: standard-setting, monitoring and implementation. These functions of

NGOs are currently expanding from a U.N. perception to a focus of NGOs which includes a broader range of international *organisations* and the transnational private sector. Perhaps most importantly, NGOs have collected the information necessary to reveal the truth about human rights conditions in the most remote or politically oppressed corners of the world. Many cases of human rights violations fall between the cracks of local, national and international systems of governance and justice; NGOs try to compensate for these gaps by invoking international human rights standards.

In recent years NGOs have taken on similar functions with respect to other international organizations. The creation of the World Bank's Inspection Panel in September 1993 is a significant example of a new mechanism created to investigate complaints made by people affected by World Bank–financed projects who allege that the bank has violated its own policies and procedures. NGOs pressured the World Bank and its political constituency to establish the panel which has monitored the Bank during its first five years in existence. The panel's mandate has clear inclusive human rights connotations, allowing it participation and recourse for people affected by the World Bank's action or inaction. Furthermore, the mandate of the panel refers to social, economic and environmental standards. While still grounding their strategies in the imperative for action as provided by U.N. human rights principles, NGOs advocate for changes in situations where local and regional realities are connected to international policy and decisionmaking processes, whether it is a World Bank loan or the involvement of a multinational corporation in a developing country like that of Shell in Nigeria.

Increased interdependence has compelled NGOs to introduce human rights standards or call for their enforcement, even where there are no immediate organizational outlets to test them. Globalization has often induced governments who are eager to safeguard a World Bank loan or a large investment by a multinational company to violate basic freedoms, encroaching upon the political space of their own civil societies.

Such conflicts cause a struggle for political space within

civil society. This space is the arena in which non-state actors may undertake initiatives independently, vis-à-vis the state. While NGOs are not the only ones affected, they tend to be at the forefront of globalizing civil societies, and therefore at the center of these discussions. Today, NGOs can formulate an organized response through their flexible relations. . . .

Making NGOs More Effective

NGOs have greatly contributed to the development of the U.N. human rights system as a normative framework. But do the increasing numbers of NGOs and NGO networks represent hope and building blocks for a system of global governance that will enforce human rights more effectively?

The answer is "yes" when we look at the ways in which NGOs and their networks promote an organizational culture within and across borders, strengthening the freedoms of association, assembly and expression in ways that open up the political space for civil societies. Responding to the forces of globalization, these new forms of civil organizations, which are able to work simultaneously across different issues and different local, national and international spaces, are absolutely necessary to effectively promote human rights and the pursuit of justice.

The answer is "no," or at best "not yet," when we review the need for NGOs to improve their own accountability vis-à-vis the people they are trying to serve and among themselves. The more NGOs take on responsibilities to provide for what should be public entitlements, the more they will need to be subject to public scrutiny. Equally, the quality of NGO relationships must reflect the universal values that NGOs promote—namely, equality of opportunity, transparency and democracy.

*"Human rights organizations have . . .
been captured by governments."*

Nongovernmental Organizations Are Increasingly Counterproductive

Robert Hayden

Since the end of the Cold War, nongovernmental organizations (NGOs) have begun to act in ways that diminish human rights, Robert Hayden contends in the following viewpoint. According to Hayden, these organizations—whose purported purpose is to safeguard human rights—have become staunch advocates of the use of force by stronger states, which can often result in human rights abuses. He also maintains that NGOs have been co-opted by governments and governmental agencies, from which they receive a large percentage of their funding; consequently, NGOs are less likely to reach independent conclusions about human rights abuses and appropriate measures to address them. Hayden is the director of the Center for Russian and East European Studies at the University of Pittsburgh.

As you read, consider the following questions:
1. As stated by the author, what were the consequences of privatization in Russia and Eastern Europe?
2. Why does Hayden consider the International Criminal Tribunal for the former Yugoslavia a "captured NGO"?
3. According to Hayden, what percentage of the American Bar Association's Central and Eastern European Law Initiative comes from the U.S. government?

Robert Hayden, "Dictatorships of Virtue?" *Harvard International Review*, vol. 24, Summer 2002. Copyright © 2002 by Harvard International Relations Council, Inc. Reproduced by permission.

With the Cold War now an almost fond memory of a good cause won, democracy should be secure in the world. Almost no political ideology opposes it. Even states in what U.S. President George W. Bush dubbed the "axis of evil" call themselves republics, leaving those few polities claiming to be emirates almost as quaint as the Hindu and Buddhist kingdoms of the Himalayas, if better endowed with money. Recent wars have been waged "out of respect for human rights" (as Vaclav Havel justified the North Atlantic Treaty Organization's (NATO) attacks on Yugoslavia) and to liberate women from oppression (as Bush partially justified U.S. attacks on Afghanistan). Protection of minorities is seen as so important that access to international organizations or to International Monetary Fund aid may be denied to countries that do not sufficiently safeguard human rights.

Yet, events since the famous victory provide opportunities to confront basic issues of democracy, sovereignty, and political accountability as well as the relationships of governments and non-governmental organizations (NGOs) to these issues. Furthermore, this new perspective allows a re-evaluation of perceptions of social events in which these issues have been confronted with some less than pleasant realities, such as in post-socialist Europe, for example.

This viewpoint casts a skeptical eye on some of the common assumptions underlying these issues and questions what usually goes without saying because it is taken as self-evident. The basic argument [is] that . . . far from weakening under globalization, major states are growing stronger. Second, NGOs tend to support strong states rather than "civil society" and also help officials avoid accountability for their actions.

The Problems of Privatization

In 1996, a dissident judge in Serbia argued that his country had suffered the worst possible transition from state socialism: the privatization of the state and the stratification of the economy. He was certainly right for Serbia, and also for much of the rest of Eastern Europe. As Janine Wedel has shown in her work *Collision and Collusion: The Strange Case of Western Aid to Eastern Europe, 1989–98*, the "privatization" of much of Russia and Eastern Europe often meant the expropriation of massive resources by local state officials, sometimes supported by Western government-sponsored "advisors." Note that this was not a matter of globalization or the weakening of the state; the existence of state structures was the main precondition for the expropriation through privatization.

At the same time that many states have been privatized in Eastern Europe, some traditionally non- or even anti-state actors in the United States and Western Europe have been co-opted by, or have themselves co-opted, other states—or both in some cases. This phenomenon is most apparent in the realm of human rights.

A Growing Support for Force

Organizations founded to criticize states' use of force have become proponents of the massive application of force by stronger states against weaker ones, since that is what "humanitarian intervention" means, at least when coupled with the realist limitation that it should be done "where we can do it," meaning without suffering losses or risking retaliation. Some human rights organizations are both explicit and triumphant about their change of role from persuasion to prosecution. A 2000 Human Rights Watch (HRW) World Report explicitly describes this shift in strategy: "Until now . . . human rights organizations could shame abusive governments. They could galvanize diplomatic and economic pressure. They could invoke international human rights standards. But rarely could they trigger prosecution of tyrants or count on governments to use their police powers to enforce human rights law. Slowly, this appears to be changing."

Prosecution, of course, is a quintessential state function, as is waging war. Prosecution is phrased deceptively in the HRW report as "using police powers," a gross misuse of a legal phrase that refers to the power of a government to maintain order within its own territory. Neither prosecution nor waging war was considered a human rights endeavor before 1999. Similarly, it has passed unnoticed that in October 2000, Amnesty International (AI) ironically called for the arrest of political figures in a joint letter with HRW and other human rights organizations to former U.S. President Bill Clinton. It cannot be argued that these organizations are themselves uninvolved in prosecutions since they actively provide support services to prosecutors. In much the same way that industries "capture" regulatory agencies and end up drafting legislation and regulations, human rights organizations have been captured by some governmental agencies.

The Structure and Expertise of NGOs

Large nongovernmental organizations (NGOs) resemble multinational corporations in structure and operation. They are hierarchical, maintain large media, government lobbying, and public relations departments, head-hunt, invest proceeds in professionally managed portfolios, compete in government tenders, and own a variety of unrelated businesses. The Aga Khan Fund for Economic Development owns the license for second mobile phone operator in Afghanistan, among other businesses. In this respect, NGOs are more like cults than like civic organizations.

Many NGOs promote economic causes—anti-globalization, the banning of child labor, the relaxing of intellectual property rights, or fair payment for agricultural products. Many of these causes are both worthy and sound. Alas, most NGOs lack economic expertise and inflict damage on the alleged recipients of their beneficence. NGOs are at times manipulated by—or collude with—industrial groups and political parties.

Sam Vaknin, "The Self-Appointed Altruists," UPI, October 9, 2002.

Yet human rights organizations have also been captured by governments. For example, the prosecutor of the International Criminal Tribunal for the former Yugoslavia (ICTY)[1] is supported by a human rights NGO called the Coalition for International Justice (CIJ). This "NGO," however, was actually founded by the US State Department. Of course, the ICTY itself may be seen as a captured NGO. While it was founded by the United Nations under a statute that requires that it be funded out of UN general funds in order to ensure its independence from individual states, the ICTY is in reality funded primarily by NATO countries. When, during the Kosovo war, NATO's spokesman was asked whether any NATO personnel feared indictment by the ICTY, he responded that "NATO is the friend of the

1. The ICTY was established in 1993 to restore peace in war-torn Yugoslavia and bring to justice people who violated humanitarian law.

Tribunal . . . NATO countries are those that have provided the finances to set up the Tribunal, we are among the majority financiers." Thus, he was "certain" that the prosecutor would only indict "people of Yugoslav nationality." His certainty seems justified thus far, as the prosecutor has said expressly that she will not prosecute NATO personnel.

NGOs Have Been Co-Opted

The stratification of NGOs may be seen in the activities of the Independent International Commission on Kosovo, an international expert group chaired by South African Constitutional Court Justice Richard Goldstone, appointed and funded by the traditionally neutral Swedish government to give a "detailed, objective analysis" of events leading up to and during the Kosovo war. This NGO chose as its legal advisor the director of the American Bar Association's Central and East European Law Initiative (ABA-CEELI), seemingly an NGO par excellence, and its U.S. meetings were organized by the "independent, nonpartisan" US Institute for Peace (USIP). Yet ABA-CEELI obtains more than 80 percent of its funding from the US government, while the USIP is solely funded by the US Congress and has the undersecretary of defense for policy and the assistant secretary of state for intelligence and research as ex officio members of its board. Perhaps not surprisingly, the Independent International Commission's conclusions on the legal implications of the Kosovo war were very similar to those of the US State Department.

The common feature of the CIJ, ABA-CEELI, HRW, AI, the ICTY, and the Independent International Commission on Kosovo is the co-optive relationship between these putatively nongovernmental organizations and national governments. It is not simply that these NGOs are parts of "transnational advocacy networks," a term suggested by Margaret Keck and Kathryn Sikkink, but rather that they have themselves been statified, co-opted into providing support services for states. Their top executives are paid accordingly, even as the lower ranks provide, in essence, volunteer work. What is interesting, however, is that this symbiosis depends on the continued vitality of states, even though state sovereignty is supposedly weakening.

Periodical Bibliography

The following articles have been selected to supplement the diverse views presented in this chapter.

Sophie Boukhari	"Child Labour: A Lesser Evil?" *UNESCO Courier*, May 1999.
Brice Dickson	"Human Rights Commissions," *Human Rights*, Summer 2000.
Catherine Edwards	"The Real Swap: Humanity for Trade," *Insight*, May 15, 2000.
Tony Evans	"If Democracy, Then Human Rights?" *Third World Quarterly*, August 2001.
Pharis J. Harvey	"Ending Abusive Child Labor," *Christian Social Action*, July/August 1999.
Andrew Hsiao	"Standing Up to the Swoosh," *Village Voice*, October 10, 2000.
Issues and Controversies on File	"Tibet," August 28, 1998.
Richard Miniter	"The False Promise of Slave Redemption," *Atlantic Monthly*, July 1999.
Joshua Muravchik	"The UN on the Loose," *Commentary*, July/August 2002.
Dara O'Rourke	"Sweatshops 101," *Dollars and Sense*, September/October 2001.
Clarence Page	"Kids Light a Candle for Human Freedom," *World & I*, June 1999.
Vijay Prashad	"Calloused Consciences," *Dollars and Sense*, September/October 1999.
N.S. Rembe	"Reflections on Human Rights Education," *Christian Social Action*, March 1999.
Michael A. Santoro	"Promoting Human Rights in China Is Good Business," *Wall Street Journal*, June 29, 1998.
Jeffrey N. Wasserstrom	"Beyond Ping-Pong Diplomacy," *World Policy Journal*, Winter 2000–2001.

CHAPTER 4

How Should the United States Respond to Crimes Against Humanity?

Chapter Preface

Despite being arguably the most powerful nation in the world, the United States often finds itself at odds with other countries and international organizations when it comes to responding to human rights violations. For example, the United States is often in conflict with the United Nations, an organization established in 1945 to help promote world peace and solve global problems, such as human rights violations, through international cooperation. Although the U.S. government was heavily involved in the development of the UN, many commentators assert that America should not look to the UN as a partner when responding to human rights abuses.

One reason given for why the United States should pursue its own solutions is that the UN gives too much credence to nations whose human rights records are highly suspect. This became especially evident in 2001, when Cuba, Libya, Saudi Arabia, Sudan, and Syria were placed on the United Nations' Human Rights Commission (UNHRC)—but for the first time, the United States was not. (The United States later regained its spot.) Many criticized this decision due to the fact that all five of the newly added nations are among the world's worst human rights offenders, according to a survey by Freedom House, an organization that promotes economic and political freedom. Joshua Muravchik, writing for *Commentary* magazine, observes that the 2002 UNHRC meeting—held without an American presence—proves the hypocrisy evident throughout the UN. According to Muravchik, the commission spent much of its time harshly criticizing Israel for its role in the Israeli-Palestinian conflict while completely ignoring the majority of the nations that were guilty of human rights abuses, such as Rwanda, Libya, Saudi Arabia, and China. Murvachik argues: "The lesson in all of this is the wisdom of American unilateralism, and the folly of submitting to any new accretion of international treaties and organizations or any further role for the UN in Middle East peace efforts."

The 2001 United Nations World Conference Against Racism (WCAR) in Durban, South Africa, has also been cited as a reason why the United States should be cautious about aligning itself with the UN. America decided not to send a delegation to the conference, which, like the UNHRC meeting, was largely anti-America and anti-Israel. Arch Puddington, the vice president at Freedom House, explains: "While the most abusive treatment was reserved for Israel, the United States was singled out for attack on a number of counts. . . . For most of those present at Durban, America was a country to be condemned, not admired—an attitude only strengthened by Washington's decision to withdraw from the WCAR in solidarity with Israel." He adds that the conference was an attack on liberal democracies, with the ethnic and racial conflicts besetting non-Western nations mostly ignored.

Whether or not it chooses to work with the United Nations or other international organizations, the United States must be involved in finding solutions to human rights abuses. In the following chapter, the authors debate different policies that the United States can adopt as it responds to crimes against humanity.

"It is in U.S. national security interests to remain positively engaged in the process of creating the court."

The United States Should Support the International Criminal Court

Washington Working Group on the International Criminal Court

In July 2002, a treaty establishing an International Criminal Court (ICC)—which would try people charged with genocide, war crimes, or crimes against humanity—took effect. Two months prior, the United States declared that it would not become a party to the treaty. In the following viewpoint, written prior to the U.S. government's decision, the Washington Working Group on the International Criminal Court asserts that the United States has serious misconceptions about the treaty and should not be afraid to support the ICC. According to the organization, the court does not violate the U.S. Constitution and will not affect the United States' ability to participate in peacekeeping missions. The Washington Working Group coordinates American non-governmental organizations that support the ICC.

As you read, consider the following questions:
1. According to the authors, what did the Clinton administration consider the only "flaw" in the ICC treaty?
2. How does the Rome Statute affect the ICC's role in peacekeeping and humanitarian missions?

Washington Working Group on the International Criminal Court, "The International Criminal Court and U.S. National Security," www.wfa.org, 2001.

The U.S. is at a critical point in policy-making on the International Criminal Court (ICC). As a signatory to the treaty, the U.S. is bound not to work against the purposes and objectives of the Treaty—as noted by Secretary of State Colin Powell in his confirmation testimony. The George W. Bush Administration and Congress must make important decisions about the U.S. position before the next Preparatory Commission (PrepCom) meeting begins at the end of February [2001]. The following points address some of its critics' most common concerns.[1]

The ICC Is Not Flawed

I. Concern: The ICC is "significantly flawed" and the U.S. should seek a full exemption from ICC jurisdiction at the negotiations.

(A) The only outstanding "flaw" in the treaty cited by the Bill Clinton Administration was the court's jurisdiction over individuals from countries that have not ratified the Treaty. However, U.S. citizens and soldiers who commit crimes abroad are currently subject to the jurisdiction of the territorial state in which the crime is committed. The ICC will have jurisdiction over the personnel of non-Party States only when these individuals commit crimes under the jurisdiction of the ICC in the territory of a State Party, or in the territory of a state that has chosen to accept the jurisdiction of the ICC. Therefore, until the U.S. ratifies the Treaty, the court can only try Americans if they commit crimes in countries that have accepted the court's jurisdiction.

(B) A report by the non-partisan American Academy of Arts and Sciences states, "Most ICC signatories reportedly see little reason to create such an exemption, which appears designed to reward non-signatories and undermine the concept that all individuals are subject to the relevant international law. It appears highly unlikely that such a "fix" will be attained. . . ."

(C) U.S. efforts for exemption are alienating our closest friends and allies, for whom the creation of a fair and effective ICC is a high foreign policy priority. During the November

1. In May 2002, the United States rescinded its support of the treaty.

2000 PrepCom, the head of the German delegation announced the German ratification of the treaty with a unanimous vote in the Bundestag. He said, "In the Bundestag debate on 27 October representatives of all parties taking the floor again emphasized the necessity to fully safeguard the integrity of the Rome Statute. The German Government was warned not to admit any changes of or exemptions from the Statute, in particular related to the jurisdiction of the Court and to cooperation with the Court. On the German side, we are confident that together, the members of the European Union, the like-minded States and all the 116 Signatory States will not fail to fully safeguard the integrity of the Statute."

(D) While efforts at exemption will not succeed, it is imperative that the U.S. has a negotiator at the table. Many important decisions on financial regulations and rules, privileges and immunities, and other aspects of the court will be made in the coming Preparatory Commission sessions. It is in U.S. national security interests to remain positively engaged in the process of creating the court.

Not a Threat to Americans

II. Concern: U.S. military and civilian personnel and officials may be subject to frivolous or politically-motivated charges by the ICC. With hundreds of thousands of soldiers deployed around the world, the U.S. would be unjustly targeted.

(A) The ICC must defer to national courts under the principle of complementarity. The court may not proceed with any case that is genuinely being investigated or prosecuted by a state which has jurisdiction, or already has been investigated by a state which has jurisdiction over it and the state has decided not to prosecute the person concerned, or the person has already been tried for the same conduct.

(B) The ICC Statute has "Made in the USA" stamped all over it. Subsequent to the conclusion of the Rome Treaty,[2] U.S. civilian and military negotiators worked to develop procedures that limit the likelihood of politicized prosecutions through greater precision in the definitions of crimes within the court's jurisdiction, among other protections. The Statute

2. The treaty was created in Rome during a 1998 UN conference.

has been enormously strengthened because of the hard work of U.S. delegations on substantive and technical issues.

(C) Any crime committed by an American would have to constitute a core crime under the ICC (genocide, crimes against humanity and war crimes) and would be subject to threshold for investigation and prosecution. All three require some sort of plan, policy or strategy to commit the crimes, and the crimes must be committed as part of a pattern of such crimes. The thresholds are so high that the United States and its official personnel could never, under U.S. law, plan and engage in such extraordinarily severe and systematic crimes.

McMillan. © 2002 by Stephanie McMillan. Reprinted with permission.

(D) The court will not acquire jurisdiction over individual crimes such as rapes, looting, or bar brawls, unless it could be demonstrated that they were the result of an official U.S. policy. Even atrocities committed by rogue units, such as the My Lai Massacre in Vietnam, would not come under the court's jurisdiction.

(E) It is already illegal for U.S. soldiers to commit the crimes that fall under the ICC's jurisdiction. According to Judge Robinson O. Everett of the U.S. Court of Military Appeals, ". . . the existing provisions of the Uniform Code of Military Justice and the War Crimes Act [of 1996] have already created jurisdiction over war crimes on the part of U.S. courts-martial . . ." He continues, "Therefore, the principle of complementarity set out in the ICC statute would provide the United States a basis for maintaining that American servicemembers accused of crimes prohibited by the Statute should be tried by a U.S. court-martial, rather than by the ICC."

The ICC Is Not Unconstitutional

III. Concern: The ICC seems unconstitutional, and does not provide for a jury trial.

(A) Even in an administration skeptical of the ICC, the U.S. Department of Justice ruled that there are no Constitutional barriers to joining the ICC.

(B) The ICC's procedural protections constitute full U.S. Bill of Rights protections for accused persons, except for jury trials. The right to jury trial in the Bill of Rights applies only to cases heard in the U.S. However, active duty members of the armed forces are not guaranteed jury trials under the U.S. Constitution. Moreover, Americans have been extradited for trial abroad for hundreds of years, even to systems without American-style justice systems. Moreover, in a July 25, 2000 statement to the House Committee on International Relations on behalf of the American Bar Association, former Assistant General Counsel for International Affairs in the Office of Secretary of Defense and Legal Adviser to the Department of State Monroe Leigh states that the Rome Statute contains full due process protections: the "Treaty of Rome contains the most comprehensive list of due process protections which has so far been promulgated."

Military Strategy Will Not Be Affected

IV. Concern: The existence of the ICC might dampen U.S. military participation in peacekeeping and humanitarian missions.

(A) The U.S. will not have to change its strategy because U.S. strategy already conforms to international and domestic law in field operations.

(B) Under the Rome Statute, the ICC must defer to agreements between states—such as U.S. Status of Forces Agreements (SOFA)—before proceeding with a request for surrender (Article 98). The U.S. almost invariably requires a SOFA or similar agreement before engaging in peacekeeping or humanitarian missions.

(C) The potential threat from the ICC is a symbolic challenge to American decisions about the use of force. The ICC will have no independent enforcement powers. The task of apprehending suspects will fall to states, which already have the authority to apprehend suspects within their borders. The UN Security Council could decide to take enforcement action, but this would be subject to a U.S. veto.

"United States participation in the ICC treaty regime would be fundamentally inconsistent with the founding principles of this country."

The United States Should Not Support the International Criminal Court

Lee A. Casey and David B. Rivkin Jr.

The treaty that established the International Criminal Court (ICC)—which would investigate, try, and punish various crimes against humanity—runs counter to the values on which the United States was founded and should not be supported, Lee A. Casey and David B. Rivkin Jr. argue in the following viewpoint. According to the authors, the treaty threatens the American ideal of self-government. In addition, they contend that the judicial system established by the ICC violates the U.S. Constitution and could place American soldiers and civilians at the mercy of judges who harbor animosity toward the United States. This viewpoint was written prior to the U.S. government's decision in May 2002 to rescind its support for the ICC. Casey and Rivkin are lawyers who worked for the Reagan and George H.W. Bush administrations.

As you read, consider the following questions:

1. What did the U.S. Supreme Court rule in *United States v. Balsys*, as stated by Casey and Rivkin?
2. According to the authors, what danger did the writers of the U.S. Constitution seek to eliminate?

O n July 17, 1998, a treaty creating a permanent International Criminal Court (ICC) to investigate, try, and punish individuals who violate certain international human rights norms was adopted at a United Nations-sponsored conference in Rome. The treaty was adopted over the objections of the U.S. delegation.

The Bill Clinton Administration rightly voted against the treaty after all its efforts to obtain even the minimum safeguards to prevent this court from being used as a political tool against the United States had been defeated. The Administration's decision, however, came late in the process, and apparently was motivated by fears that prosecutions might be brought against U.S. peacekeepers overseas, not by the realization that the permanent ICC concept itself is fundamentally flawed.

An Abusive System

As outlined in the Rome treaty, the ICC's powers are an open invitation to abuse. The crimes under the jurisdiction of the ICC are broadly defined and could subject individuals to penalties of up to life imprisonment for actions that never were thought punishable on the international level before. Cases could be brought before the court based upon the complaint of any country that ratifies the ICC treaty (an "ICC States Party") or the initiative of the court's prosecutor—an international independent counsel. Once indicted, individual defendants would be tried by a bench of judges chosen by the ICC States Parties. As an institution, the ICC would act as police, prosecutor, judge, jury, and jailer. All of these functions would be performed by its staff, or under its supervision, with only bureaucratic divisions of authority. The court would be the sole judge of its own power, and there would be no process to appeal its decisions, however irrational or unjust those might be.

Unfortunately, merely refusing to join the Rome treaty will not protect Americans from the ICC's reach. In an astonishing break with the accepted norms of international law, the Rome treaty would extend the ICC's jurisdiction to the citizens of countries that have not signed and ratified the treaty. Consequently, if 60 other countries ratify this treaty, the ICC will be established in the Netherlands with the power to try and punish Americans, even if the United States does not sign or ratify it. As a result, the United States can protect its citizens only by actively opposing ratification of the ICC treaty by 60 states; this would prevent the ICC's establishment. . . .

Reasons to Oppose the ICC

As adopted, the ICC treaty is an unchecked invitation to abuse and use as a political tool to restrain America's ability to defend its interests. Although the Clinton Administration refused to approve the ICC treaty, it has indicated that it might change its position if certain revisions were made. In fact, numerous non-govermental organizations (NGOs) and members of the Like-Minded Group [a coalition of 130 African, Asian, Latin American, and Eastern European countries] are pressing the Administration to move in that direction.

However, even if the treaty were amended to incorporate measures that protect U.S. troops on peacekeeping missions from prosecution, it would remain both legally and politically inimical to the interests of the United States. Specifically:

• The ICC threatens American self-government. The creation of a permanent, supranational court with the independent power to judge and punish elected officials for their official actions represents a decisive break with fundamental American ideals of self-government and popular sovereignty. It would constitute the transfer of the ultimate authority to judge the acts of U.S. officials away from the American people to an unelected and unaccountable international bureaucracy. As Alexis de Tocqueville wrote in his *Democracy in America*, "[h]e who punishes the criminal is . . . the real master of society."

In this regard, the claims of ICC supporters that the court is not directed at American citizens may be dismissed. Suggestions that U.S. soldiers and civilians could not be brought before the ICC because that court would be required to defer to U.S. judicial processes—the concept of "complementarity"—are disingenuous. Under the ICC treaty, the court would be the absolute judge of its own jurisdiction and would itself determine when, if ever, such a deferral was appropriate.

American Tradition Is Ignored

• The ICC is fundamentally inconsistent with American tradition and law. In its design and operation, the ICC is fundamentally inconsistent with core American political and legal values. Indeed, if Americans ever were arraigned before the ICC, they would face a judicial process almost entirely foreign to the traditions and standards of the United States.

First and foremost, they would face a civil law "inquisitorial" system where guilt would be determined by judges (possibly from countries hostile to the United States) alone. There would be no right to trial by jury, a right considered so central by the Founders of the American Republic that it was guaranteed twice in the U.S. Constitution (in Article III, Section 2, and the Sixth Amendment).

The Separation of Powers

The American concept of the separation of powers reflects the settled belief that liberty is best protected when, to the maximum extent possible, the various authorities legitimately exercised by government are placed in separate branches. So structuring the national government, the Framers believed, would prevent the excessive accumulation of power in a limited number of hands, thus providing the greatest protection for individual liberty. Continental European constitutional structures do not, by and large, reflect a similar set of beliefs. They do not so thoroughly separate judicial from executive powers, just as their parliamentary systems do not so thoroughly separate executive from legislative powers. That, of course, is entirely their prerogative, and substantially explains why they are more comfortable with the International Criminal Court's (ICC) structure, which so closely melds prosecutorial and judicial functions. They may be able to support such an approach, but we should not.

John R. Bolton, *National Interest*, Winter 1998–1999.

Trial by jury is not, of course, the only right guaranteed to Americans that would be unavailable in an ICC. For example, an American surrendered to the ICC would not enjoy rights to reasonable bail or a speedy trial, as those rights are known and guaranteed in the United States. Although the ICC would have to provide a trial "without undue delay," this could mean many years in prison. For instance, mocking the presumption of innocence, the prosecutor of the United Nations International Criminal Tribunal for the Former Yugoslavia, a court widely viewed as a model for the ICC, actually argued that up to five years would not be too long to wait *in prison* for a trial.

In addition, the fundamental right of a defendant to confront the witnesses against him and to challenge their evidence would be fatally compromised in the ICC. The "international" rule and practice is quite different. In the U.N. Yugoslav Tribunal, both anonymous witnesses and extensive hearsay evidence (where the witness cannot be challenged) have been allowed at criminal trials. Moreover, the ICC prosecutor would be able to appeal a verdict of acquittal, effectively placing the accused in "double jeopardy." Such appeals have been forbidden in the law of England and the United States since the 17th century. If convicted, the defendant would be unable to appeal the verdict beyond the ICC itself, and could be consigned to a prison in any one of the States Parties to the treaty at the ICC's pleasure and under its supervision.

The ICC Violates the Constitution

• The ICC violates constitutional principles. The failure of the ICC treaty to adopt the minimum guarantees of the U.S. Constitution's Bill of Rights is, in fact, one of the principal reasons why the United States could not, even if it wanted to, join the ICC treaty regime.

As the U.S. Supreme Court recently suggested in *United States v. Balsys*, the United States cannot participate in or facilitate a criminal trial under its own authority, even in part, unless the Constitution's guarantees are preserved. If, however, the United States were to join the ICC treaty regime, the prosecutions undertaken by the court, whether involving the actions of Americans in the United States or overseas, would be "as much on behalf of the United States as of" any other State Party. Since the guarantees of the Bill of Rights would not be available in the ICC, the United States could not participate in, or facilitate, any such court.

United States participation in the ICC treaty regime would also be unconstitutional because it would allow the trial of American citizens for crimes committed on American soil, which are otherwise entirely within the judicial power of the United States. The Supreme Court has long held that only the courts of the United States, as established under the Constitution, can try such offenses. The Supreme Court made this clear in the landmark Civil War case of *Ex parte Milligan*. In that case, the Court reversed a civilian's conviction in a military tribunal, which did not provide the guarantees of the Bill of Rights, holding that "[e]very trial involves the exercise of judicial power," and that the military court in question could exercise "no part of the judicial power of the country." This reasoning is equally applicable to the ICC.

American Principles

• The ICC contradicts the founding principles of the American Republic. United States participation in the ICC treaty regime would be fundamentally inconsistent with the founding principles of this country. The Declaration of Independence, which articulates the principles that justify the American Republic's very existence, listed the offenses of the King and Parliament that required separation from England, revolution, and war. Prominent among those offenses were accusations that Britain had (1) subjected Americans "to a jurisdiction foreign to our constitution and unacknowledged by our laws"; (2) "depriv[ed] us, in many cases, of the benefits of Trial by Jury"; and (3) "transport[ed] us beyond [the] Seas to be tried for pretended offences."

These provisions referred to the British practice of prosecuting Americans in "vice-admiralty" courts for criminal violations of the navigation and trade laws. Like the ICC, these courts followed the civil law, "inquisitorial" system. Convictions, of course, could be obtained far more easily from these tribunals than from uncooperative colonial juries. The U.S. Constitution's Framers sought to eliminate forever the danger that Americans might again be surrendered to a foreign power for trial by specifically requiring that criminal trials be by jury and conducted in the state and district where the crime was committed. This is the only right guaranteed by the Constitution to be stated twice in the original document and its first ten amendments. As Justice Joseph Story explained, the "object" of these provisions was "to secure the party accused from being dragged to a trial in some distant state, away from his friends, and witnesses, and neighborhood; and thus subjected to the verdict of mere strangers, who may feel no common sympathy, or who may even cherish animosities, or prejudices against him."

Of course, if the United States were to join the ICC treaty, Americans again would face transportation beyond the seas for judgment, without the benefits of trial by jury, in a tribunal that would not guarantee the other rights they take so much for granted and where the judges may well "cherish animosities, or prejudices against" them.

"Hesitancy to ratify [the Convention on the Elimination of All Forms of Discrimination Against Women] stems from unfounded fears."

The United States Should Ratify the Convention on the Elimination of All Forms of Discrimination Against Women

Amnesty International

In the following viewpoint, the worldwide human rights organization Amnesty International asserts that the United States should ratify the Convention on the Elimination of All Forms of Discrimination Against Women (CEDAW), a treaty that sets worldwide standards on women's equality. The organization maintains that America's failure to support CEDAW is based on several fallacies. According to Amnesty International, CEDAW will not supersede American law or lead to a sharp increase in lawsuits. In addition, Amnesty International contends that despite the claims of people who do not want the U.S. Senate to ratify the convention, CEDAW will not impose liberal views concerning sexuality on U.S. citizens.

As you read, consider the following questions:
1. According to Amnesty International, how does CEDAW define "discrimination"?
2. Why do the authors dispute the claim that the convention will usurp the role of parents?
3. Why does CEDAW have no effect on same-sex marriages, as stated by Amnesty International?

Amnesty International, "Fear vs. Fact," www.amnestyusa.org, November 1999.
Copyright © 1999 by Amnesty International USA. Reproduced by permission.

The United States is a world leader in the promotion of women's rights, particularly in giving meaning to the principle of the equality of women and men. Nevertheless, the U.S. has not ratified the authoritative document that sets comprehensive standards on women's equality, the Convention on the Elimination of All Forms of Discrimination against Women (CEDAW). Although as of November 1999, 165 countries had ratified this Convention, the U.S. remains in the company of countries like Iran and the Sudan, where women's rights are in a deplorable state. [The treaty remained unratified as of December 2002.] In part, hesitancy to ratify this important document stems from unfounded fears associated with the implementation of CEDAW in the U.S. These fears are addressed below:

The Effects of Ratification

FEAR: U.S. ratification of CEDAW would give too much power to the international community with the provisions of the Convention superseding U.S. federal and state law.

FACT: As with many international agreements, countries can express "reservations, understandings and declarations" in cases where there are discrepancies between the international convention or treaty and domestic law. For the most part, U.S. law complies with the requirements of the Convention and the Convention is compatible with the principles of the U.S. Constitution. And, where any differences do exist, the Convention calls for appropriate measures to be taken to progressively promote the principle of nondiscrimination. CEDAW grants no enforcement authority to the United Nations.

FEAR: Ratifying CEDAW would authorize individuals to file an avalanche of lawsuits to enforce it.

FACT: As the treaty would be considered by the Senate it would not authorize any lawsuit not already authorized by U.S. law. Full implementation of CEDAW's standards over time could increase U.S. protections against discrimination, but this would require separate action by Congress and the Administration subject to U.S. checks and balances and consistent with all U.S. constitutional protections.

FEAR: "Discrimination" is too broadly defined in CEDAW

and its implementation in the U.S. would result in unwise laws and "frivolous" lawsuits.

FACT: CEDAW's definition of discrimination includes both discrimination which is intentional and that which is the result of laws, policies, and practices which, when applied, have the impact of discriminating against women. U.S. law already governs discrimination in private and public employment, prohibiting policies and practices that unintentionally burden women greater than men. Regardless, claims in the U.S. related to sex discrimination are not subjected to the same "strict scrutiny" standards applied to claims of race discrimination. Thus, full legislative implementation of CEDAW could help to rectify these discrepancies in U.S. law over time. Because there has been no flurry of frivolous lawsuits since U.S. ratification of the UN Convention to Eliminate All Forms of Racial Discrimination (CERD), there is no reason to expect them upon U.S. ratification of CEDAW either.

CEDAW Will Not Destroy Families

FEAR: CEDAW can be used to destroy the traditional family structure in the U.S. by redefining "family" and the respective roles of men and women.

FACT: CEDAW does not, and would not, seek to regulate any constitutionally protected interests with respect to family life. Both CEDAW and the U.S. Constitution recognize the restraints of any governing authority to interfere with an individual's most basic decisions regarding family. CEDAW simply urges State Parties "to adopt education and public information programmes, which will eliminate prejudices and current practices that hinder the full operation of the principle of the social equality of women." How best to implement this obligation would be considered by the U.S. authorities consistent with the protections of the U.S. Constitution.

FEAR: Implementation of CEDAW would usurp the proper role of parents in child-rearing.

FACT: CEDAW simply calls for a recognition of the "common responsibility of men and women in the upbringing and development of their children" and maintains that

Because the local/national/domestic and the global/international are mostly seen as separate spheres, we often have trouble determining what local actions will have the greatest impact globally. Thus, for example, there has been little interest [in the United States] in using international human rights treaties like the Convention on the Elimination of All Forms of Discrimination Against Women (CEDAW) to advance domestic issues. There is a tendency not to see the international arena as adding anything to causes at home. But just as women's global networking and international solidarity have helped sustain feminist activists who are isolated in their home countries, US feminists can benefit from the support of women elsewhere, which we will need if we are to challenge what is now openly defended as the American Empire.

Charlotte Bunch, *The Nation*, September 23, 2002.

"the parents' common responsibility [is] to promote what is in the best interest of the child." The U.S. Constitution limits the power of government to interfere in certain private matters such as decisions by parents concerning the upbringing of their children. CEDAW implementation would not change this fact. Moreover, determining a child's "best interest" is a matter which U.S. courts consider already in extreme cases involving violence, abuse, abandonment, and neglect.

Education and Sexuality

FEAR: CEDAW may discourage or eliminate single-sex schools and/or force local school districts to "gender neutralize" school textbooks and programs.

FACT: CEDAW does not require the prohibition of single-sex education, but, does encourage States Parties to support co-education as well as other types of education which may achieve the aim of educational equality. This language is particularly meant to address the needs of many countries which, unlike the U.S., have yet to develop educational programs which are accessible to both young girls and boys. In terms of its application to the U.S., CEDAW would encourage the development of equal educational material, whether taught in single-sex or mixed schools, but it does not prohibit single-sex schools.

FEAR: CEDAW supports abortion through its promotion of access to "family planning."

FACT: Actually, CEDAW does not address the matter of abortion and, according to U.S. State Department reports, is "abortion neutral." Many countries in which abortion is illegal—such as Ireland, Burkina Faso and Rwanda—have ratified CEDAW.

FEAR: U.S. ratification of CEDAW might be used to sanction same-sex marriages.

FACT: The Convention makes clear that it is aimed only at discrimination that is directed specifically against women. A same-sex marriage claim would include a charge that both men and women who want to marry individuals of their own sex are being discriminated against. There is no provision in the Convention that would compel the U.S. Congress to pass same-sex marriage laws in order to comply.

VIEWPOINT

*"Western women . . . went to Beijing
hoping to advance a world view which
insists that all women need liberation from
their families."*

The United States Should Not Ratify the Convention on the Elimination of All Forms of Discrimination Against Women

Kathryn Balmforth

In the following viewpoint, Kathryn Balmforth asserts that the United States should not ratify the Convention on the Elimination of All Forms of Discrimination Against Women (CEDAW) because the treaty is part of the continued efforts of radical Western feminists to force their political agenda on the rest of the world. She argues that these feminists have tried since the 1995 United Nations World Conference on Women to impose their deleterious definition of women's rights, which include disparaging motherhood and opposing responsible sexual behavior, on all nations. According to Balmforth, CEDAW would result in intrusive governments bent on modifying human conduct. Balmforth is a civil rights attorney and the former director of the World Family Policy Center.

As you read, consider the following questions:
1. In the author's view, how do women from developing nations define "equality"?
2. Why does Balmforth disagree with the term "sex worker"?
3. What do most people assume is the purpose of human rights treaties, according to the author?

Kathryn Balmforth, "Beijing Plus Five: Deconstructing the UN Conference on Women," *Ex Femina*, April 2000, pp. 8–10. Copyright © 2000 by Independent Women's Forum, www.iwf.org. Reproduced by permission.

To women from the developing world who attended the Beijing Conference on Women [in 1995], "equality" means equal access to education, food, and health care, and the right to participate in politics and business. To radical Western feminists and lesbian rights activists, the term "equality" is much more malleable.

A Radical Feminist Agenda

These Western women already enjoy equal access to food, education, health care, politics, and business. They went to Beijing hoping to advance a world view which insists that all women need liberation from their families, and that all women should be fully employed outside the home, because the only things worth doing are those which can be quantified and measured in economic terms.

While the activists were attempting to create new human rights in controversial areas like autonomous sexual freedom for minor children, they were also attempting to denigrate long-established rights which stood in their way—rights to family privacy, the right of parents to direct their children's upbringing, particularly their religious and moral up-bringing, rights of conscience and religious freedom, and the right of peoples to determine their own political destinies.

These Western activists—and their governments—en-countered stiff opposition from the developing world, and eventually, the traditional family was reaffirmed as the basic unit of society.

Undaunted, Western radicals have utilized the non-binding Beijing Platform for Action as a tool in their continuing effort to create a new, unagreed upon, yet binding, human rights agenda.

Radical activists are coordinating the "reinterpretation" of existing binding human rights treaties along lines allegedly suggested by the Beijing language. This process is largely occurring in the two human rights "treaty bodies" most influenced by the feminists—the committee administering the Convention on the Elimination of All Forms of Discrimination Against Women (the "CEDAW Committee"), and the Human Rights Committee, which administers the International Covenant on Civil and Political Rights.

Vague Language and Stereotypes

These committees appear to be implementing only the vague language favored by the radicals, ignoring balanced language which was carefully negotiated at Beijing, and interpreting the vague language to imply rights expressly rejected at Beijing.

Even the right to sell one's body is included in the radical interpretation of "reproductive rights," as China was instructed by the CEDAW Committee to legalize prostitution. Prostitutes are now referred to as "sex workers," connoting that prostitution is just another job.

Usurping the Parental Role

The Convention on the Elimination of All Forms of Discrimination Against Women (CEDAW) undercuts the proper role of parents in child rearing. Articles 5 and 16 affirm that in family matters "the interests of the children shall be paramount." Who decides what is in a child's "best interest"? What penalty would result from violating the "best interest" of the child? This superficial, feel-good statement subordinates every family member, regardless of the issue or circumstance.

Regarding children's interests, CEDAW conveys that government, not parents, knows best. The Committee derided Slovenia because only 30 percent of children under age three were in day-care centers. The remaining 70 percent, the committee claimed, would miss out on education and social opportunities offered in day-care institutions. Its review of Germany urged "the Government to improve the availability of care places for school-age children to facilitate women's re-entry into the labor market."

The Committee even seeks to empower governments to usurp parents' role in teaching values to their children. In its report on Romania, it encouraged "the Government to include sex education systematically in schools." It has called for the same action in other countries.

Laurel Macleod and Catherine Hurlburt, "Exposing CEDAW," September 5, 2000, http://cwfa.org.

The Beijing Platform for Action calls for the elimination of stereotypes. But the only stereotype routinely targeted is motherhood. Governments are ridiculed for portraying motherhood as a "noble" calling. One government was criticized because only 30 percent of its tiniest children—those under three years of age—were in day care, while the rest were being cared for by their families. The only document in which motherhood was given unqualified encouragement was one in which a European government was admonished to make certain that lesbians were not denied access to artificial insemination.

At an earlier UN conference known as Cairo Plus Five, the United States delegation made repeated surreptitious efforts to remove the words "responsible sexual behavior" from a list of topics adolescents should be taught, to be replaced by simply teaching "sexuality." Finally, the delegation of the Holy See [the office of the pope asked], "What does the delegation of the United States have against responsible sexual behavior?"

An Intrusive Treaty

The Clinton administration has pressed for United States ratification of CEDAW [as of December 2002, the treaty had not been ratified]. This would make all the radical pronouncements of the CEDAW committee binding upon the United States. Furthermore, while most people assume that "human rights" treaties are meant to protect us from oppressive, intrusive government, CEDAW does the opposite. It contains language calling for the most intrusive government imaginable. It requires governments to "modify the social and cultural patterns of conduct of men and women, with a view to achieving the elimination of prejudices, customs, and all other practices which are based on . . . stereotyped roles for men and women."

However, the fact that we have not ratified CEDAW does not necessarily insulate Americans from its effects. Some American courts have begun incorporating United Nations human rights standards into American law.

*"The U.S. government's refugee policy
could, quite literally, mean the difference
between life and death for substantial
numbers of individuals each year."*

The United States Should Admit More Refugees Suffering Serious Human Rights Abuses

Mark Gibney

The United States must do more to help refugees, Mark Gibney claims in the following viewpoint. He argues that America's refugee policy is still mired in the Cold War practice of admitting mostly refugees from Communist nations. Since the Cold War is over, the United States should instead focus on providing a temporary haven for individuals living under the most brutal circumstances, no matter what country they originate from, he asserts. According to Gibney, such a change would help the United States make a greater contribution toward the cause of human rights. Gibney is the Belk Professor of Political Science at the University of North Carolina at Ashville and the author of *Strangers or Friends: Principles for a New Alien Admission Policy.*

As you read, consider the following questions:
1. According to Gibney, how many refugees did the United States admit during the first half of the 1990s?
2. What does the author believe is the greatest strength of a "burden sharing" refugee policy?
3. In Gibney's opinion, what do the problems in the U.S. alien admission policy reflect?

Mark Gibney, "In Search of a U.S. Refugee Policy," *The United States and Human Rights: Looking Inward and Outward*, edited by David P. Forsythe. Lincoln: University of Nebraska Press, 2000. Copyright © 2000 by University of Nebraska Press. Reproduced by permission.

In theory, there are very few ways in which it would be possible for the United States to make a more positive contribution to the world than through the admission of refugees. Without attempting to sound melodramatic, the U.S. government's refugee policy could, quite literally, mean the difference between life and death for substantial numbers of individuals each year. And at the risk of sounding hopelessly naive, I would argue that perhaps there is no purer way for the United States to protect the human rights of others than through a refugee admission policy that focused on meeting the needs of the most desperate among us.

In fact, the United States has, on one level at least, been very generous in terms of the number of refugees it has admitted. During the 1980s the United States admitted nearly 1 million refugees and close to 600,000 for the first half of the 1990s. Particularly for a Western country, these numbers are extraordinarily high. The problem is that the United States has not necessarily been admitting refugees through its overseas refugee admission program, as evidenced by the relatively mild forms of persecution in nearly all the countries where refugees are migrating from. Thus, I would argue, the United States has been admitting "immigrants" but labeling these individuals "refugees." Although there is nothing wrong with admitting immigrants as such, the appropriate manner for doing so is by some other means (such as through normal flow immigration channels). Admitting immigrants as refugees not only cheapens the concept of refugeehood, but much more importantly, it thereby deprives others—real refugees—of an opportunity for safety in this country.

The Need for a New Policy

For decades, U.S. refugee policy has served the ends and the goals of American foreign policy. This was certainly true before 1980 when refugee admissions were limited by law to individuals from communist countries or from the Middle East (although nearly all were from the former). Refugees fleeing communist regimes were taken as proof positive of the evils of those regimes and the superiority of our way of life. The 1980 Refugee Act offered the promise of some change, but this opportunity was missed.

The promotion of ideological solidarity is a commendable goal for U.S. foreign policy and perhaps for refugee admissions as well. The problem—at least in terms of refugee admissions—is that by the 1980s the worst abuses of communist rule had long been over. To be sure, all these countries were governed by repressive regimes, and nearly all the population suffered the daily indignities and duplicities of life in a communist country. But with virtually no exception these were not countries marked by large-scale political violence. Still, the United States readily responded to this repression but in doing so essentially ignored the claims of millions of individuals who were brutalized by far more violent regimes. Whatever justification there may have been at one time for focusing U.S. refugee policy on the claims of individuals from communist countries has certainly passed by now. The Cold War is over; the Lautenberg Amendment[1] expired in 1996. It is time to create a new U.S. refugee policy.

The term "burden sharing"[2] receives a lot of attention in the refugee literature, but it is a term essentially devoid of meaning because it is a concept in search of implementation. Consider, however, an American refugee policy that was premised on the concept of burden sharing and which made a concerted effort to protect those in grave danger. Under such a policy we could admit, say, 40,000 refugees a year. This would be a sharp reduction in the numbers we currently take in and even 10,000 below the baseline established under present law. The difference is that we would be admitting real refugees as opposed to disguised immigrants. One means of achieving this would be to actively recruit (for lack of a better term) those in the most desperate of circumstances. This, after all, is why we grant individuals refugee status in the first place. However, rather than granting permanent residence to those taken in, as we do presently (which is another indication of the lack of distinction between immigrants and refugees under present policy), we should instead only offer a temporary safe haven until danger has passed.

1. The amendment required that historical persecution be considered when determining whom to accept as refugees.   2. Which postulated that nations should share the responsibility when responding to large-scale refugee influxes.

What are the advantages of this kind of refugee system? To point out the obvious, the proposal's greatest strength is that it would reduce human misery in a way that present policy seldom does. Quite obviously, the United States cannot admit anywhere near the number of people who are in need of such assistance, but this is also a manner in which we could (safely) become involved in some of the worst human crises on the planet. Imagine, for example, if the United States had offered a safe haven to several thousand Rwandan refugees, either during the 1994 genocide, or at any time since then. What would this accomplish? The most important would be that thousands of people would be given safety—a safety that did not (and presently does not) exist. Beyond this, however, such an involvement also would have provided the United States (along with the other Western countries) the opportunity, as well as the impetus, to begin to address the political quagmire that gave rise to this utter brutality in the first place. Would this ensure a lessening of ethnic tension, or would it mean that hostilities would not persist? Of course not. But, I would argue, it would have represented a much better policy—politically as well as morally—than the one that we have pursued—which has been little more than to sit back and watch the horror unfold.

Potential Problems

A number of objections would be made to the proposal outlined above. One is that in admitting a substantially different "class" of refugees, there would be far more difficult problems of assimilation than we presently face. This much is conceded. However, with temporary admission the norm (and permanent residence the exception), the assimilation of refugees is not a goal to be pursued, at least not initially. Related to that, another objection might be that, based on the apparent lack of political willpower to deport unsuccessful asylum applicants, any "temporary" admission of refugees would easily turn into something like we have at present: permanent residence. This, however, is due in large part to poor administration, an unfortunate hallmark of the Immigration Service. This should not be a reason for not attempting to create a refugee system.

Why Refugees Should Be Welcomed

There are compelling moral and economic arguments why more people from poor countries should be allowed to move to rich ones. The world has made the movement of goods, money and ideas freer, but not, strangely, the movement of people. It is both right to give desperate people sanctuary and rewarding to welcome new citizens. History has shown that immigrants bring ideas, vigour and ambition, as well as their mere labour. Some welcome debate has begun on this issue. Mexico's president, Vicente Fox, has made a good start with George W. Bush, on the role of guest-workers in America. The president of the European Commission, Romano Prodi, recently highlighted Europe's need for foreign labour. And some countries are adopting more flexible attitudes albeit because of a rather narrow problem: a skills shortage.

Economist, March 31, 2001.

The strongest objection to such a proposal may be that it threatens to create a further "mess" in this country's alien admissions—and don't we have enough going on in this area already? Though I would most definitely agree with the premise, I do not accept the conclusion. U.S. alien admission policy has certainly been ill conceived, but this is also a reflection of how it has attempted to be all things to all people: to employers who enjoy cheap labor, to families who wish to be reunited in this country (but who could, in most instances, be reunited back in the home country), to a public that wants the benefits of aliens without the presence of aliens, to well-entrenched interest groups who promote admission of their own "refugee" group only, and so on.

Because of this, I suspect that little will change. We will, most certainly, make stronger efforts to prevent illegal aliens from entering and working here; but, we will make no real effort to deal with the reasons why they are flocking here in the first place. We will continue to placate those who have family members who wish to migrate to the United States, as well as the needs of the business community, although the numbers might well decline in the short run. What will not be questioned, however, is the 10:1 ratio of immigrants to refugees, a policy that somehow seems to be etched in stone.

We can point to the cruelty of the 1938 *St. Louis* incident[3] without realizing that we are doing essentially the same thing now. Humanitarianism is nice in theory but apparently has severe limits in practice. In sum, U.S. alien admission policy, for all intents and purposes, will pretty much stay its present course. All I would ask for, then, is for a U.S. refugee policy that makes a much deeper contribution to the cause of human rights in the world than the one that we have at present.

3. A boat named the *St. Louis* containing 930 Jewish refugees was denied admittance to the United States.

"*Refugee resettlement has grown into a substantial public/private enterprise directly employing thousands and equaling if not exceeding the U.S. foreign aid budget in its demands for public money.*"

Admitting More Refugees into the United States Is Too Costly

Don Barnett

In the following viewpoint, Don Barnett contends that America's refugee policy has become little more than an economic boon to both the refugees and the voluntary agencies that are supposed to help refugees adjust to life in America. According to Barnett, the millions of dollars given to these agencies are rarely used to help refugees find employment and become integrated into their new communities. Instead, Barnett argues that these agencies spend most of their time placing refugees in welfare programs. He concludes that America's refugee policy is costing Americans too much money. Barnett is a writer who specializes in immigration and refugee issues.

As you read, consider the following questions:
1. How much money do the two largest voluntary agencies receive each year, according to Barnett?
2. What does the author consider "a reversal of the traditional notions of citizenship"?
3. According to Barnett, what has replaced persecution as the chief cause of refugee migration?

P rior to the mid-1970s, refugee sponsorship was mostly the work of private charities, but with the Refugee Act of 1980 public funds have dominated all aspects of refugee resettlement. Even in the 1980s and early 1990s the Private Sector Initiative program allowed sponsoring organizations to bring over refugees if they were willing to cover costs of resettlement and support after arrival, but Voluntary Agencies (Volags), preferring to lobby for increased government support of refugees, shunned the private program and it was discontinued in 1995 for lack of use. Public money always drives out private money. Put another way by a state refugee official at the [1999 office of Refugee Resettlement] conference who asked not to be named: "Volags only do what the state pays for." The two largest Volags—U.S. Catholic Charities and the Hebrew Immigrant Aid Society—together received about $75 million in State Department and Office of Refugee Resettlement (ORR) funds for their U.S. operations alone in 1996, the last year for which data is available, and a Volag affiliate boasts in a publication that money "pours" in from local and state governments as well.

A Lack of Responsibility

Naturally this money is meant to be used to help refugees. But the Volags have astonishingly meager responsibilities for actual resettlement and support of the refugees they sponsor. The Volags do not even guarantee the federal loans made to the refugees for airfare to the United States. (Less than half of the loans made for this purpose since the 70's have been paid back, leaving an unpaid bill of $415 million.) Judging from this conference, their main function is to get refugees on federal welfare programs as soon as possible.

Every refugee resettled in the United States is assigned to one of 10 Volags, adding to that agency's headcount and therefore federal cash allotment. In many cases the Volag's responsibility for the refugees it sponsors is virtually nil, though in fairness it must be noted that a Volag often has little choice over individuals assigned to it. Refugee recruitment largely takes place independently of both the Volags and the U.S. government.

Cheryl Smith, director of Sacramento County Social Services, describes a Pentecostal church that expands its membership through missionary activity in Ukraine. The church members are initially placed in cities around the United States by the State Department and the Volags. But with their true destination the community that first contacted them, the religious refugees quickly undertake a second migration to Sacramento, leaving the Volag "sponsor" a mere observer rather than a participant with a stake in the process. In the case of the Pentecostal church, the pastor, church leadership, and most of the members are dependent on welfare, as is the whole informal refugee sponsorship network, in this case it was Pentacostals, but according to the FBI about 2,000 Russian organized crime operatives had been sponsored into the country on the refugee program by 1996. (Another 2,000 arrived illegally.)

Refugees and Welfare

Citizenship was the theme of [the conference]. Promoted in clinics paid for with tax dollars, it was touted as a way to maintain access to federal benefit programs. Refugees are exempt for seven years from the bar on welfare usage that applies to other new immigrants. After seven years, they must become citizens in order to maintain access to some federal benefits. State and local agencies prefer dependence on federal programs over dependence on local programs. Accordingly, both private and governmental agencies use tax dollars in citizenship drives for everything from coaching to transportation and Immigration and Naturalization Services (INS) processing fees. Mass mailings inform noncitizen welfare recipients of the need to naturalize in order to avoid losing their entitlements. State programs, such as the Massachusetts Citizenship Assistance Program, target those "who are receiving state-funded benefits that could be replaced with federal benefits were they to become citizens." The state has set up a 24-hour hotline to reach this segment of the population with its message about the advantages of citizenship.

Recognizing the new value of citizenship, the Volags have also leveraged their tax dollars to promote citizenship—U.S. Catholic Charities uses Americorp staff for the task. One agency offers a brochure on how to qualify as disabled for purposes of taking the simplified citizenship exam in one's own language. In a reversal of traditional notions of citizenship, the more mentally incompetent the applicant is, the easier it is to gain citizenship.

Legally, refugees and asylees are eligible for all welfare on the same basis as U.S. citizens within 30 days of arrival. (Asylees are those who are already in the United States when they seek the right of permanent U.S. residency based on a claim that they would be persecuted if returned home.) A 1996 federal study of refugees arriving in the previous five years found that 46 percent of refugee households were receiving cash assistance. Approximately 48 percent of the households received food stamps. About 12 percent of refugee households were in public housing with possibly another 12 percent on waiting lists for public housing or Section 8 housing. These figures are quite startling in view of the fact that 75 to 80 percent of refugee arrivals are joining family members who settled in previous waves.

Total welfare usage by refugees cannot be determined. Three years after welfare reform, however, there are about 203,000 noncitizen refugees and their children receiving federal cash assistance through Temporary Assistance to Needy Families (TANF) and/or Supplemental Security Income (SSI) in California alone. No one knows the number of citizen refugees receiving federal cash assistance in California because it is not tracked, but it could be equal to or greater than the number of dependent noncitizen refugees. Further, based on studies that track welfare usage for five years after arrival, refugees typically use local general assistance cash at even higher levels than either TANF or SSI. California is home to about a quarter of the nation's refugees. Generalizing to the rest of the nation is risky, but the California data suggest that substantial long-term welfare dependence is the norm for many refugees. Without welfare there would be no refugee resettlement program as we know it.

No Incentive for Integration

Dismantling private sponsorship has changed the basic assumptions that guaranteed the integrity of earlier refugee resettlement. First, it obviated the need to integrate refugees as soon as possible into the language, economy, and host community. The usual incentives and disincentives do not function when cash, food, housing, and medical care are available upon arrival. Perhaps most importantly it has induced many to immigrate who otherwise would never have entertained the notion, furthering the development of enclaves of those who cannot or will not assimilate. It also raised politics and management of public opinion to new levels—"controlling the agenda" was one of the themes at [1999's] conference. At a strategy session of refugee advocates and publicists at another conference I attended, an attorney leading the session explained that winning public opinion and congressional support depended on controlling the terms of the debate. Fencing discussion in with a framework of "refugees" who are always "fleeing for their lives" shuts down the opposition every time. When I pointed out that the very use of the term "refugee" for most of those entering on the refugee program was an example of controlling and defining the terms of the debate he readily agreed, and went on to say that many staffers at his own resettlement agency refuse to use the term "refugee" and pointedly refer to the new arrivals as "those people."

There needn't be any worry over media treatment of the subject. Such reporting as there is consists mainly of stories about mistreatment of individuals at the hands of the immigration system. The overwhelming impression from media accounts, for instance, is that asylee flows have been choked down to a trickle by draconian new laws and that innocent applicants are being thrown in jail or deported to life threatening situations at home. The *New York Times*, analyzing a six-month period of immigration data, reported in June of 1998 that "from August of last year through the end of January" 1,300 new arrivals expressed a fear to return home. Of those, 1066 were sent to detention; the rest were deported." Nowhere does the article state that this data relates only to the tiniest source of asylum applications—those who show up at airports without valid documents and file for asylum. Most asylum seekers apply after their temporary visas expire or after successfully entering the country on bogus documents. In fact, about 59,000 new applications for asylum were made in 1997. This represents about 88,500 individuals, far exceeding the expected flow implied in the law and not including an additional 30,000 whose applications from previous years were reconsidered under appeal. Annual asylum applicants exceed the number implied in the *Times* article by a factor of 34. Less than 5 percent of asylum applicants are ever held in detention and those that are spend an average of less than three months in detention. In addition, they have the right to withdraw their applications and return home at any time.

The Age of Refugees

County of Origin	Under 5 Years	School Age (5–17)	Working Age (16–64)	Retirement Age (= or > 65)
Former Yugoslavia	9.0	25.4	67.9	1.7
Former Soviet Union	8.5	26.7	58.2	10.6
Iran	5.3	21.6	74.5	2.9
Sudan	6.7	21.7	80.8	0.2
Somalia	6.1	35.2	64.2	4.0
Liberia	9.2	40.9	56.1	1.8
Vietnam	12.9	13.6	74.7	1.3
Afghanistan	7.0	46.6	51.3	2.3
Cuba	6.2	17.4	72.5	6.5
Iraq	9.4	28.5	63.8	2.1
Sierra Leone	5.2	33.7	64.6	4.5
Ethiopia	4.2	27.7	79.1	0.6
Burma	19.5	14.5	66.7	0.9
Togo	3.6	32.2	68.8	0.4
Dem. Rep. Congo	13.3	42.2	50.8	0.0
All Other Countries	11.8	33.7	59.0	0.2

*Totals may exceed 100% due to overlapping age categories.

U.S. State Department, *Proposed Refugee Admission for FY 2003*, 2002.

If public discussion of the refugee program skims from one cliché to the next, writings not meant for public consumption reveal a Hobbesian [a reference to philosopher Thomas Hobbes] struggle for influence over the program. A Russian activist group, in a 1998 appeal to members about the forthcoming "battle for the refugee quota" writes: "Lobbyists from Asian countries and Eastern Europe (particularly those from Poland) are seeking to bring in their own people in order to increase the size of their ethnic groups; it's the same picture when it comes to distributing federal, state, and local government resources. We need 'warriors' with legal and administrative skills and experience in American government who are dedicated to the community." As reported by the *Washington Forward*, the then Democratic Counsel for the House immigration subcommittee, Marina Hone, whose office wants more African refugees, says "One thing that has struck us are the disparities and inconsistencies in U.S. immigration law. . . . If we want a system that is a fair and unambiguous system, we need refugee allocations that are roughly proportional to the population on the ground." Alluding to the "battle for the refugee quota," she goes on to say that "folks would like to see the black community and the Jewish community at odds over this and it's not happening. No one thinks you need to help Africans at the expense of helping Soviet Jews." The *Forward* also reports that a black-Jewish crisis could occur if the quota of one group was lowered to accommodate the demands of the other group, hence agreement on all sides to work together to increase the overall quota. Assistant Secretary of State for the Bureau of Population, Refugees, and Migration Julia Taft announced at [1999's] conference that the refugee resettlement would henceforth be more diverse and representative of the world's refugees.

A Gigantic Enterprise

Both refugee and asylee numbers have already vastly outstripped all projections made when the 1980 Refugee Act was signed. Public sponsorship allowed numbers to go much higher than would have been possible with private sponsorship and removed all effective controls over the process except for the political. Maybe that's why in most cases group preferences and family-chain migration have replaced persecution as the engine of refugee migration to the United States.

In fiscal year 1998, about 77,000 refugees were resettled permanently to the United States, not including 20,000 Cubans who arrived with most of the same rights and entitlements as refugees. Additionally, though final numbers are unavailable, new applications for asylum were filed for at least 80,000 individuals in 1998. (These figures do not include recent "one-time" amnesties for 200,000 Central Americans, Cubans and Haitians, temporary protected status for certain nationals who have overstayed their visas, or smaller humanitarian immigration programs.)

In a December 1998 letter to the State Department, Senator Spencer Abraham, Senate immigration subcommittee chair, along with Senators Orrin Hatch, Ted Kennedy, and Patrick Leahy, argued for a refugee flow of 90,000 to 100,000 (not including Cubans and other humanitarian admissions) as it reflects "America's great traditions" and represents a small proportion of overall immigration anyway. The main Volags are calling for a refugee admission ceiling of 111,000, an increase of 44 percent over current numbers, arguing in part that larger numbers are necessary to justify overhead and staff in the private charities.

Many of the jobs they are trying to protect are held by the new arrivals themselves. Refugee resettlement has grown into a substantial public/private enterprise directly employing thousands and equaling if not exceeding the U.S. foreign aid budget in its demands for public money when the cost of long-term public assistance is counted. Indeed the private and the public are hardly distinguishable. Julia Taft, formerly the director of the consortium of private charities requesting an increase in the annual refugee quota, is now the director of the State Department bureau that makes the U.S. government's recommendation for that quota. According to federal and state sources, the second in charge at ORR recently left his government job for a position as the Executive Vice President at the largest resettlement agency, at an annual salary in excess of $200,000 per year.

There is nothing new about a federal program that has gone off the tracks. The circular arrangements that make the refugee program work characterize many of our public institutions, but few share the refugee program's potential to so radically change America.

Periodical Bibliography

The following articles have been selected to supplement the diverse views presented in this chapter.

Henri Astier — "Rights of the Despised," *American Prospect*, August 14, 2000.

William Bauer — "A Time for Tough Measures," *Maclean's*, August 23, 1999.

Liberato C. Bautista — "The Case for an International Criminal Court," *Christian Social Action*, July/August 1998.

John R. Bolton — "Courting Danger," *National Interest*, Winter 1998–1999.

The Economist — "Let the Huddled Masses In," March 31, 2001.

Don Feder — "Human Rights Not a Foreign Policy Concern," *Conservative Chronicle*, March 20, 2002.

Russ Feingold — "Human Rights: Crucial to U.S. Foreign Policy," *Christian Science Monitor*, February 11, 1998.

David Moberg — "A New Interventionism," *In These Times*, February 7, 2000.

Bill Richardson — "America's Interest in an International Court," *The New York Times*, August 21, 2001.

Alfred P. Rubin — "Some Objections to the International Criminal Court," *Peace Review*, March 2000.

Annys Shin — "Who's Afraid of the International Criminal Court?" *In These Times*, September 6, 1998.

Christine Stolba — "The Beijing Brigade," *Women's Quarterly*, Winter 2000.

Tim Wichert — "People on the Move," *A Common Place*, November 1999.

For Further Discussion

Chapter 1

1. Blair Gibb and John A. Gentry are critical of the American definition of human rights, contending that the U.S. emphasis on individual rights and Americans' wrongful sense of entitlement are harmful to national cohesion and lead to economic stratification. Do you believe that these claims are fair, or do you think that America's understanding of human rights has been wrongfully denigrated? Explain your answer.

2. Do you agree with William Ratliff's assessment of bias by human rights organizations such as Amnesty International? What steps, if any, do you think these organizations must take in order to be credible to people of all political views?

3. After reading the viewpoints by the World Health Organization and Richard D. Lamm, do you think that health care should be a universal human right, or are the economic costs too high? Can the idealism of human rights coexist with the fact that some of these rights, such as health care and access to a decent-paying job, are often out of reach for economically unstable nations? Explain your answers.

Chapter 2

1. Michael Byers and Richard Lowry disagree on whether the Geneva Convention applies to the detainees held at Guantánamo Bay. Whose argument do you find more convincing and why? Do you think that any violations of the convention, if they occurred, were justified in the wake of the September 11, 2001, terrorist attacks? Why or why not?

2. Do you agree with Scott Rubush's assertion that sweatshops provide important political and economic benefits to Third World nations, or do you believe that any such advantages are outweighed by the reported mistreatment of those factory workers? Explain your answer.

3. Temma Kaplan asserts that activists have played an important role in making the rest of the world aware of human rights abuses against women and girls in developing nations. Do you believe that human rights abuses can only be wholly understood by the victims, or can outsiders accurately judge the state of human rights? Explain your answer.

Chapter 3

1. After reading the viewpoints by Peter van Tuijl and Robert Hayden, do you believe that nongovernmental organizations can help improve human rights, or have they become too dependent on governments? Why or why not?

2. Charles Jacobs suggests that African slavery has been ignored by human rights organizations because the perpetrators are not white. Do you believe this is a fair assessment? Explain your answer.

3. Fred Smith and others who oppose economic sanctions against sweatshops maintain that those factories are important to the economy of Third World nations. What do you believe should take precedence: the human rights of workers or economic opportunities? Since the right to work is considered a basic human right, can sanctions that might close sweatshops and eliminate jobs be considered human rights violations? Explain your answers.

Chapter 4

1. After reading the viewpoints in this chapter, what do you believe are the most important steps that should be taken by the United States in order to protect human rights? What actions should the United States take that were not mentioned by the authors? Explain your answers.

2. Do you agree with Amnesty International's argument that the Convention on the Elimination of All Forms of Discrimination Against Women (CEDAW) will not threaten American families, or do you believe Kathryn Balmforth is correct when she asserts that CEDAW will impose radical feminist views in the United States and throughout the world? Explain your answers.

3. After reading the viewpoints by Mark Gibney and Don Barnett, do you believe the U.S. refugee policy should be reformed? Why or why not? If so, how do you think the policy can best be improved? Explain your answers.

Organizations to Contact

The editors have compiled the following list of organizations concerned with issues debated in this book. The descriptions are derived from materials provided by the organizations. All have publications or information available for interested readers. The list was compiled on the date of publication of the present volume; the information provided here may change. Be aware that many organizations take several weeks or longer to respond to inquiries, so allow as much time as possible.

American Anti-Slavery Group (AASG)
198 Tremont St., #421, Boston, MA 02116
(800) 884-0719
e-mail: info@iabolish.com • website: www.iabolish.com

The American Anti-Slavery Group is a grassroots organization dedicated to combating slavery around the world. AASG has helped free over forty-five thousand slaves since its founding in 1993. The iAbolish web-portal serves as AASG's Internet presence and features articles and interviews with activists and freed slaves.

American Civil Liberties Union (ACLU)
132 W. 43rd St., New York, NY 10036
(212) 944-9800 • fax: (212) 869-9065
e-mail: aclu@aclu.org • website: www.aclu.org

The ACLU is a national organization that works to defend Americans' civil rights as guaranteed by the U.S. Constitution. It works to establish equality before the law, regardless of race, color, sexual orientation, or national origin. The ACLU publishes and distributes policy statements and pamphlets on topics such as the death penalty, as well as the semiannual newsletter *Civil Liberties Alert* and the annual *International Civil Liberties Report.*

Amnesty International (AI)
322 Eighth Ave., New York, NY 10001
(212) 807-8400 • fax: (212) 473-9193 or (212) 627-1451
e-mail: admin-us@aiusa.org • www.amnestyusa.org

Amnesty International is a worldwide, independent voluntary movement that works to promote internationally recognized human rights. It also aims to free people detained for their beliefs who have not used or advocated violence and people imprisoned because of their ethnic origin, sex, language, national or social origin, economic status, birth, or other status. AI seeks to ensure fair and prompt trials for political prisoners and to abolish torture, "disappearances," cruel treatment of prisoners, and executions. Its publications include a quarterly newsletter, *Amnesty Action*; an annual book, *Amnesty International Report*; and documents on a wide variety of human rights issues, such as the death penalty, women's issues, refugees, and prisoners of conscience. The organization also publishes various briefing papers and special reports.

Canadian Human Rights Foundation (CHRF)
1425 René-Lévesque Blvd. West, Suite 407, Montréal, Québec, Canada H3G 1T7
(514) 954-0382 • fax: (514) 954-0659
e-mail: chrf@chrf.ca • website: www.chrf.ca

The Canadian Human Rights Foundation is a nonprofit, nongovernmental organization dedicated to defending and promoting human rights in Canada and around the world. Its programs educate people on human rights laws and support the development of democratic civil society. The CHRF also holds conferences on human rights issues and publishes on topics such as refugees and migrant workers. The CHRF also publishes the bilingual newsletter, *Speaking About Rights*.

Child Labor Coalition (CLC)
c/o National Consumers League
1701 K St. NW, Suite 1200, Washington, DC 20006
(202) 835-3323 • fax: (202) 835-0747
e-mail: childlabor@nclnet.org • website: www.stopchildlabor.org

The CLC serves as a national network for the exchange of information about child labor. It provides a forum for groups seeking to protect working minors and to end the exploitation of child labor. It works to influence public policy on child labor issues, to protect youths from hazardous work, and to advocate for better enforcement of child labor laws. The CLC publishes advocacy alerts and reports on child labor. The website also offers the *Online Monitor*, an electronic news service that provides domestic and international child labor news.

The Federation for American Immigration Reform (FAIR)
1666 Connecticut Ave. NW, Washington, DC 20009
(202) 328-7004 • fax: (202) 387-3447
e-mail: info@fairus.org • website: www.fairus.org

FAIR is a national organization that believes the mass immigration that has occurred over the past several decades should be curtailed. FAIR supports a temporary moratorium on immigration, with exceptions for a limited number of refugees and the spouses and minor children of U.S. citizens, and supports the development of a nondiscriminatory immigration policy. The organization publishes the monthly newsletter *Immigration Report* and an annual report.

Human Rights Watch
350 Fifth Ave., 34th Fl., New York, NY 10118-3299
(212) 290-4700 • fax: (212) 736-1300
e-mail: hrwnyc@hrw.org • website: www.hrw.org
Human Rights Watch regularly investigates human rights abuses in more than seventy countries around the world. It promotes civil liberties and defends freedom of thought, due process, and equal protection under the law. Its goal is to hold governments accountable for human rights violations they commit against individuals because of their political, ethnic, or religious affiliations. It publishes the annual *Human Rights Watch World Report* and reports on human rights in dozens of nations, children's rights, women's rights, and war.

International Campaign for Tibet (ICT)
1825 K St. NW, Suite 520, Washington, DC 20006
(202) 785-1515 • fax: (202) 785-4343
e-mail: info@savetibet.org • website: www.savetibet.org
ICT is a nonpartisan, nonprofit organization dedicated to promoting human rights and democratic freedoms for the people of Tibet. It sponsors fact-finding missions to Tibet, works in conjunction with the UN and U.S. Congress to protect Tibetan culture, and promotes educational and media coverage of human rights issues in Tibet. ICT publishes two newsletters, the *Tibet Press Watch* and the *Tibetan Environment & Development News*.

International Labour Office (ILO)
4, route des Morillons, CH-1211 Geneva 22, Switzerland
+41.22.799.6111 • fax: +41.22.798.8685
Washington Branch Office: (202) 653-7652 or (202) 653-7687
e-mail: ilo@ilo.org or washington@ilo.org • website: www.ilo.org
The ILO works to promote basic human rights through improved working and living conditions by enhancing opportunities for those who are excluded from meaningful, salaried employment. The ILO pioneered such landmarks of industrial society as the eight-hour workday, maternity protection, and workplace safety regulations. It runs the ILO Publications Bureau, which publishes various policy statements and background information on all as-

pects of employment; among these publications are *World Employment* and *Child Labour: Targeting the Intolerable.*

National Mobilization Against Sweatshops (NMASS)
NMASS, PO Box 130293, New York, NY 10013-0995
(718) 625-9091 • fax: (718) 625-8950
e-mail: nmass@yahoo.com • website: www.nmass.org
The National Mobilization Against Sweatshops (NMASS) is a grassroots organization dedicated to building a new national labor movement and changing the sweatshop system. NMASS supports the forty-hour workweek, eight-hour workdays, and the fight for a living wage. In addition to the twice yearly newsletter *Sweatshop Nation*, articles are available on the NMASS website.

National Network for Immigrant and Refugee Rights (NNIRR)
310 Eighth St., Suite 303, Oakland, CA 94607
(510) 465-1984 • fax: (510) 465-1885
e-mail: nnirr@nnirr.org • website: www.nnirr.org
The network includes community, church, labor, and legal groups committed to the cause of equal rights for all immigrants. These groups work to end discrimination against and unfair treatment of illegal immigrants and refugees. The network aims to strengthen and coordinate educational efforts among immigration advocates worldwide. It publishes a quarterly newsletter, *Network News*, along with reports and information packets.

Prevent Genocide International
e-mail: info@preventgenocide.org
website: www.preventgenocide.org
Prevent Genocide International is a nonprofit educational organization that seeks to eliminate genocide. The organization uses the Internet to educate and bring people together in order to encourage global action. A monthly *News Monitor* is issued on the website.

United Nations Association of the USA (UNA-USA)
801 Second Ave., 2nd Fl., New York, NY 10017-4706
(212) 907-1300 • fax: (212) 682-9185
e-mail: info@unausa.org • website: www.unausa.org
UNA-USA is the largest grassroots foreign policy organization in the United States and the nation's leading center of policy research on the UN and global issues. It works with the UN to identify better ways in which the international community can use its re-

sources to respond to pressing human needs, such as international terrorism, emergency relief, and human rights. It publishes the quarterly newsletter *The Inter Dependent*, the annual book *A Global Agenda: Issues Before the General Assembly of the United Nations*, and fact sheets on issues such as U.S./UN relations and the International Criminal Court.

Bibliography of Books

Marjorie Agosín, ed.   *A Map of Hope: Women's Writings on Human Rights.* New Brunswick, NJ: Rutgers University Press, 1999.

Marjorie Agosín, ed.   *Women, Gender, and Human Rights: A Global Perspective.* New Brunswick, NJ: Rutgers University Press, 2001.

Omer Bartov, Atina Grossmann, and Mary Nolan, eds.   *Crimes of War: Guilt and Denial in the Twentieth Century.* New York: New Press, 2002.

Gary Jonathan Bass   *Stay the Hand of Vengeance: The Politics of War Crimes Tribunals.* Princeton, NJ: Princeton University Press, 2000.

Yves Beigbeder   *Judging War Criminals: The Politics of International Justice.* New York: St. Martin's Press, 1999.

Neil Chippendale   *Crimes Against Humanity.* Philadelphia: Chelsea House Publishers, 2001.

Fred Dallmayr   *Achieving Our World: Toward a Global and Plural Democracy.* Lanham, MD: Rowman & Littlefield, 2001.

Jack Donnelly   *International Human Rights.* Boulder, CO: Westview Press, 1998.

Robert F. Drinan   *The Mobilization of Shame: A World View of Human Rights.* New Haven, CT: Yale University Press, 2001.

Michael Dummett   *On Immigration and Refugees.* London: Routledge, 2001.

Conor Foley   *Global Trade, Labour, and Human Rights.* London: Amnesty International, 2000.

Foreign Policy Association   *. . . And Justice for All: The Universal Declaration of Human Rights at Fifty.* New York: Foreign Policy Association, 1998.

David P. Forsythe, ed.   *The United States and Human Rights: Looking Inward and Outward.* Lincoln: University of Nebraska Press, 2000.

Mary Ann Glendon   *A World Made New: Eleanor Roosevelt and the Universal Declaration of Human Rights.* New York: Random House, 2001.

Richard J. Goldstone   *For Humanity: Reflections of a War Crimes Investigator.* New Haven, CT: Yale University Press, 2000.

Nelien Haspels and Michele Jankanish, eds.	*Action Against Child Labour.* Geneva: International Labour Office, 2000.
John G. Heidenrich	*How to Prevent Genocide: A Guide for Policymakers, Scholars, and the Concerned Citizen.* Westport, CT: Praeger, 2001.
Arthur C. Helton	*The Price of Indifference: Refugees and Humanitarian Action in the New Century.* Oxford, UK: Oxford University Press, 2002.
Human Rights Watch	*Fingers to the Bone: United States Failure to Protect Child Farmworkers.* New York: Human Rights Watch, 2000.
Human Rights Watch	*Uncertain Refuge: International Failures to Protect Refugees.* www.hrw.org/reports/1997/gen3.
Aleksandar Jokic, ed.	*War Crimes and Collective Wrongdoing: A Reader.* Malden, MA: Blackwell Publishers, 2001.
Craig Kielburger	*Free the Children: A Young Man's Personal Crusade Against Child Labor.* New York: HarperCollins, 1998.
Miriam Ching Yoon Louie	*Sweatshop Warriors: Immigrant Women Workers Take on the Global Factory.* Cambridge, MA: South End Press, 2001.
Mahmood Mamdani, ed.	*Beyond Rights Talk and Culture Talk: Comparative Essays on the Politics of Rights and Culture.* New York: St. Martin's Press, 2000.
Kurt Mills	*Human Rights in the Emerging Global Order: A New Sovereignty?* New York: St. Martin's Press, 1998.
Makau Mutua	*Human Rights: A Political and Cultural Critique.* Philadelphia: University of Pennsylvania, 2002.
Robert G. Patman, ed.	*Universal Human Rights?* New York: St. Martin's Press, 2000.
Hilary Poole, ed.	*Human Rights: The Essential Reference.* Phoenix, AZ: Oryx Press, 1999.
Jonathan Power	*Like Water on Stone: The Story of Amnesty International.* Boston: Northeastern University Press, 2001.
Geoffrey Robertson	*Crimes Against Humanity: The Struggle for Global Justice.* New York: New Press, 2000.
Obrad Savic, ed.	*The Politics of Human Rights.* London: Verso, 1999.
Jeremy Seabrook	*Children of Other Worlds: Exploitation in the Global Market.* London: Pluto Press, 2001.

Kirsten Sellars	*The Rise and Rise of Human Rights.* Stroud, UK: Sutton, 2002.
James D. Seymour and Richard Anderson	*New Ghosts, Old Ghosts: Prisons and Labor Reform Camps in China.* Armonk, NY: M.E. Sharpe, 1998.
Claude E. Welch Jr., ed.	*NGOs and Human Rights: Promise and Performance.* Philadelphia: University of Pennsylvania Press, 2001.
Aristide R. Zolberg and Peter M. Benda, eds.	*Global Migrants, Global Refugees: Problems and Solutions.* New York: Berghahn Books, 2001.

Index

abortion, 173
Abzug, Bella, 90
Adidas, 83, 85
Afghanistan, 98
AFL-CIO, 86
Africa, 102–103
  human rights abuses against women
    in, 92, 99, 102–103
  see also slavery
Age of Enlightenment, 12
Ainina, Hindou Mint, 120
Alemán, Arnaldo, 77
Aleu, Akec Tong, 119
Aleu, Aleu Ayieny, 119
American Anti-Slavery Group (AASG),
  118, 120, 121–22, 123
American Bar Association's Central and
  Eastern European Law Initiative
  (ABA-CEELI), 151
Amish, the, 138
Amnesty International, 169
  political bias by, 59, 60
  on slave trade, 113
  on terrorist detainees, 69, 70
Anderson, George M., 127
Annan, Kofi, 59
Apparel Industry Partnership, 81
asylum seekers, 187, 188–89, 190–91

Bahá'í International Community, 53
Balmforth, Kathryn, 174
Bangor, Maine, 131
Barnett, Don, 184
Beijing Platform for Action, 93–94,
  175, 176
Beijing Women's Conference (1995),
  91–92, 93
Bellamy, Carol, 114, 115
Bill of Rights (British), 13
Bill of Rights (U.S.), 12, 13–14
black slavery. *See* slavery
Bolton, John R., 165
boycotts. *See* consumer boycotts
Brazil, 104
Brody, Brach, 45
Bunch, Charlotte, 172
Byers, Michael, 67

Cairo Plus Five, 177
Calabrisi, Guido, 41
Canada, 46
Casey, Lee A., 162
Center for Women and Global
  Leadership, 91, 94, 95
de Chand, David, 122
children

labor by, 85, 129–30, 138
rearing of, 171–72, 176
in slavery, 113–14
violence against, 34
China
  Japanese atrocities against, 61–62
  religious persecution in, 65
  trade sanctions on, 109–10
  on Universal Declaration of Human
    Rights, 28
  World Trade Organization
    admittance and, 109
Christian Solidarity International, 113,
  115, 118, 121
de Chungara, Domitila Barrios, 91
circumcision, female, 101
citizenship, U.S., 186–87
civil rights
  Asian countries on, 28–29
  defined, 27
  Eastern European countries on,
    20–21
  vs. economic/social/cultural
    freedoms, 17–18
  nongovernmental organizations and,
    143–44
  West on, 20
Clean Clothes Campaign, 131–32
Clinton administration, 157, 163, 164
Coalition for International Justice
  (CIJ), 150
Cochrane, Archie, 46–47
Conference of Nongovernmental
  Organizations (CONGO), 94
consumer boycotts
  damage from, 136–37
  do not work, 135
  early triumphs of, 125–26
  effecting industry codes of conduct,
    128–29
  examples of, 131–32
  global awareness and, 126–27
  lack of massive participation and,
    127–28
  real motivation for, 138–39
  successful influence of, 128
Convention on the Elimination of All
  Forms of Discrimination Against
  Women (CEDAW), 144
  as abortion neutral, 173
  does not prohibit single-sex
    education, 172
  family status laws and, 103
  global feminism and, 172
  human rights activist accountability
    and, 96

is an intrusive treaty, 177
nations that have ratified, 92
radical feminist agenda and, 175–77
same-sex marriage laws and, 173
as undercutting proper role of
    parents in child rearing, 176
    con, 171–72
U.S. fears on effects of, 170–71
U.S. hesitancy on ratifying, 170
will not destroy traditional family
    structure, 171
Convention on the Rights of the Child,
    144
Crossroads Christian Communications,
    119

Declaration of Independence, 12, 13
Declaration of the Rights of Man and
    Citizen, 12, 14
Depro Provera, 78
developing world. See Third World
Dinka tribe, 113–15
discrimination
    defined in CEDAW, 170–71
    in health care, 36–37
    national origin and, 105
Donnelly, Jack, 19

Eastern bloc countries, 33
Eastern Europe, 148–49
education
    right to, 34
    single-sex, 172
Edwords, Fred, 14
Egypt, 99, 105
Eibner, John, 113, 114
El Salvador, 78
Ethical Trading Initiative, 80
Ethiopia, 100
European Parliament, 100
Everett, Robinson O., 160

factory labor. See sweatshops
Fay, Michael, 30
feminism
    global, 172
    radical, 175
First World. See United States; West,
    the
First World Conference of Women
    (1975), 91
FLAM (Forces pour la Liberation des
    Africains Mauritaniens), 120–21
FoulBall Campaign, 132
Freedom House, 154
French Constituent Assembly, 12
Friedan, Betty, 91
Fuchs, Victor, 41–42

Gap, the, 129
Garzon, Baltasar, 59–60
Geneva Convention, 68, 73, 75
genital mutilation, 101, 112–13
Gentry, John A., 49
Germany, 158
Ghana, 103
Gibb, Blair, 26
Gibney, Mark, 178
globalization
    child labor and, 130
    feminism and, 172
    nongovernmental organizations and,
        143, 146, 149
    sweatshop labor and, 86
Glorious Revolution (1688), 12–13
Golodner, Linda F., 124
Gomes, Lena, 101
Guantánamo Bay. See terrorist
    detainees
Guatamala, 99

Hague Convention (1907), 75
Hammarberg, Thomas, 17–18
Hayden, Robert, 147
health care, 33–34
    discrimination in, 36–37
    dual challenge in setting limits on, vs.
        expanding, 41
    elements combining human rights
        with, 37–39
    focusing on health vs., 46–47
    human rights as a standard for
        evaluating, 39
    limited resources for, 41–42
    prioritizing needs for, 43–44
    related to other human rights, 35–36
    right to, 34–35
        con, 42–43, 47–48
    setting limits for, 44–46
Hebrew Immigrant Aid Society, 185
Hecht, David, 120–21
HIV/AIDS, 103
Hoile, David, 117
Honduras, 78, 79
human rights
    civil/political vs. social/economic,
        17–18
    connection between health and,
        33–35
    defined, 33
    development of concept of, 12–14
    international law and, 33
    organizations
        changing role of, 149
        passivity of, on slavery issue,
            115–16
        political bias by, 59–62
        shift in strategy of, 149–50

205

MacEoin, Gary, 76
Machakos peace protocol, 118
Macleod, Laurel, 176
al-Magd, Kamal Abu, 30
Maginnis, Robert L., 74
Magna Carta, 12
Malaysia, 28, 102
maquila industry. *See* sweatshops
marriage, 102–104
  same-sex, 173
Massachusetts Citizenship Assistance
  Program, 186
Mauritania, 120–21
media
  on refugees/asylum seekers, 188
  on slave trade and redemption,
    118–20, 122–23
Menchu, Rigoberta, 60–61
Mexico, 77
Miniter, Richard, 121
morality
  relativism and, 21–22
  universality of, 20
Morocco, 103, 104
Morris, Kit, 87
Mosaic Group, 121
Muravchik, Joshua, 154

National Consumers League (NCL),
  125–26, 131
National Industrial Recovery Act
  (1933), 126
National Islamic Front (NIF), 112
NATO (North Atlantic Treaty
  Organization), 148, 150–51
NGOs. *See* nongovernmental
  organizations
Nicaragua, 78
Nigeria, 99, 103
Nike, 80–81, 83, 84–85
Nobel Peace Prize (1992), 60–61
nongovernmental organizations
  (NGOs)
  development projects and, 143
  as establishing a human rights system,
    144–46
  have been co-opted, 151
  increase in, 142
  increasing effectiveness of, 146
  relationships among, 142
  relationship to NATO, 150–51
  structure and expertise of, 150
  see also human rights, organizations
North Olmstead, Ohio, 132

Office of Refugee Resettlement (ORR),
  185
Organization for Economic
  Cooperation and Development

(OECD) Directory of NGOs, 142
organizations. *See* human rights;
  nongovernmental organizations

Pakistan, 99
persecution, religious, 65–66
Peru, 100
Phillips–Van Heusen *maquila*, 80
Pinochet, Augusto, 59, 60
Ponnuru, Ramesh, 61
PricewaterhouseCoopers, 84–85
prisoners of war (POWs), 68, 73–75
  see also terrorist detainees
privacy, right to, 34
privatization, 148–49
progressivism, 136–37

al-Qaeda, 73, 74

Ratliff, William, 58
Red Cross, 69
Reebok, 80–81, 83, 128
refugees
  admission of
    increase in, 190–91
    labeling "immigrants" as "refugees"
      for, 179
    lack of responsibility for, 185–86
    as a private/public enterprise, 191
    quotas and, 189–90
    reasons for welcoming, 182
    sponsoring organizations for, 185
    statistics, 179
  age of, 189
  asylum applications and, 188–89
  citizenship and, 186–87
  federal benefit programs for, 186
  lack of incentive for integration of,
    187–88
  media on, 188
  as temporary, 180
    advantages of, 181
    potential problems with, 181–82
  U.S. policy on
    "burden sharing," 180
    focus on Communist countries,
      179–80
    lack of change in, 182–83
  welfare and, 187
relativism, 21–22, 24
responsibility, personal, 53, 55–57
rights
  defined, 17, 18, 27
  group, vs. individual rights, 53–54
  political, 50
  see also civil rights; human rights
Rivkin, David B., Jr., 162
Robbin, Christopher, 42–43
Robinson, Mary, 34–35

Rome treaty, 163
Rubush, Scott, 82
Rumsfeld, Donald, 68

Saudi Arabia
  religious persecution in, 65–66
  violation of women's rights in, 98–99
Scott, T. Jeffrey, 143
Seabrook, Jeremy, 85
Seguine, Joel, 87–88
Serbia, 148
Shulz, William, 60
Sierra Leone, 103
Sikkink, Kathryn, 151
Singapore, 28, 30–31
Sirico, Robert A., 109
slavery
  fates of slaves under, 112–13
  investigation of, 112
  nations that have not eliminated, 114
  passivity by human rights groups on,
    115–16
  redemption of slaves
    buying back slaves, 113, 115
    as encouraging the slave trade, 121
    fraud of, 118–22
    groups involved in, 118
    media on, 122–23
    UNICEF response to, 113–15
  Sudanese Arabization and, 112
Slavery Convention (1926), 27
Smith, Cheryl, 185–86
Smith, Fred, 133
social security, right to, 34
South Africa, 99
State Consultative Council of Egypt,
  105
Stauber, John, 122
Stoll, David, 60, 61
Stop Sweatshop campaign, 131
Sudan
  religious persecution in, 65
  slavery in, 112–14, 118, 122
Sudan Campaign, 122
Sudanese People's Liberation Army
  (SPLA), 119, 122
sweatshops
  benefits of, 84–86
  child labor and, 129–30
  fighting union formation in, 80
  finding workers for, 78
  firing workers in, 78
  future of, 80–81
  intolerable working conditions in, 77,
    79
  lack of government regulation of,
    79–80
  number of, 78
  student protests against, 127

backlash against, 87–88
reasons for, 83–84
wages in, 77, 79
see also consumer boycotts
Syria, 99, 102, 103

Taft, Julia, 190, 191
Taiwan, 110
Taliban, the, 73, 74, 98
Task Force to End Sweatshops, 80
terrorist detainees
  applying customary law to, 75
  are not legitimate prisoners of war,
    73–75
  determining status of, 68–69
  human rights violations of, 70
  questionable treatment of, 68, 69–71
  upholding human rights of, 71
Tharoor, Shashi, 23
Third World
  approach to human rights, 20, 21
  benefits of labor in, 84–85
  child labor and, 134
  see also sweatshops
torture, 34
trade
  free, 109–10
  sanctions, 109
transnational companies. See
  sweatshops
treaties. See Convention on the
  Elimination of All Forms of
  Discrimination Against Women;
  International Criminal Court;
  Universal Declaration of Human
  Rights

Uganda, 103
UN Earth Summit (1991), 90–91
UNICEF (United Nations Children's
  Fund), 113–15
Union of Needletraders, Industrial, and
  Textile Employees (UNITE), 86, 131
unions, labor, 80, 86
Union Summer, 86
United Nations
  on civil/political rights vs. economic/
    social/cultural freedoms, 17
  conflict with U.S. over response to
    human rights abuses, 154–55
  Universal Declaration of Human
    Rights ratified by, 14
  WCAR, 100, 154–55
United Nations Development
  Programme (UNDP), 142
United Nations' Human Rights
  Commission (UNHRC), 154
United Nations International Criminal
  Tribunal, 166